Vegetables and Salads

Marshall Cavendish London & New York

Edited by Isabel Moore

Published by
Marshall Cavendish Publications Limited
58 Old Compton Street,
London W1V 5PA

© Marshall Cavendish Limited 1973, 1974, 1975, 1976, 1977

This material was first published by
Marshall Cavendish Limited
in the partwork *Supercook*.

First printing 1976
Second printing 1977

Printed by Henri Proost, Turnhout, Belgium

ISBN 0 85685 165 5

Contents

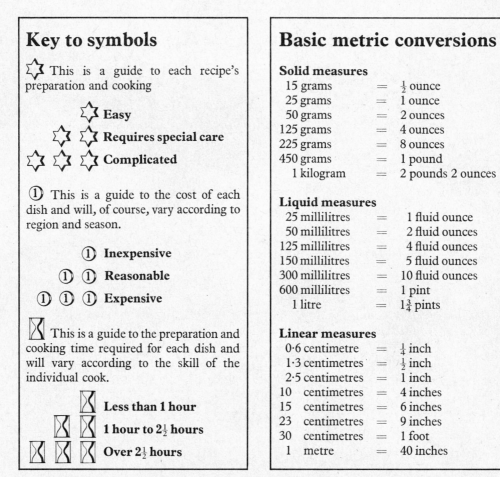

Key to symbols

☆ This is a guide to each recipe's preparation and cooking

☆ **Easy**

☆ ☆ **Requires special care**

☆ ☆ ☆ **Complicated**

① This is a guide to the cost of each dish and will, of course, vary according to region and season.

① **Inexpensive**

① ① **Reasonable**

① ① ① **Expensive**

⧖ This is a guide to the preparation and cooking time required for each dish and will vary according to the skill of the individual cook.

⧖ **Less than 1 hour**

⧖ ⧖ **1 hour to 2½ hours**

⧖ ⧖ ⧖ **Over 2½ hours**

Basic metric conversions

Solid measures

15 grams	=	½ ounce
25 grams	=	1 ounce
50 grams	=	2 ounces
125 grams	=	4 ounces
225 grams	=	8 ounces
450 grams	=	1 pound
1 kilogram	=	2 pounds 2 ounces

Liquid measures

25 millilitres	=	1 fluid ounce
50 millilitres	=	2 fluid ounces
125 millilitres	=	4 fluid ounces
150 millilitres	=	5 fluid ounces
300 millilitres	=	10 fluid ounces
600 millilitres	=	1 pint
1 litre	=	1¾ pints

Linear measures

0·6 centimetre	=	¼ inch
1·3 centimetres	=	½ inch
2·5 centimetres	=	1 inch
10 centimetres	=	4 inches
15 centimetres	=	6 inches
23 centimetres	=	9 inches
30 centimetres	=	1 foot
1 metre	=	40 inches

American equivalents of food and measurements are shown in brackets.

Vegetables and salads for the family

Vegetables and Salads were traditionally served as accompaniments to meat, fish or other 'main' dishes. Now, however, with the cost of meat and fish escalating, they are coming into their own. And variety has never been better — vegetables once considered 'exotic' and 'foreign' (and sometimes suspect!) are rapidly becoming more available, more familiar and less expensive, with beneficial effects upon our diet.

The difficulty was to decide what to include and, in the end, a compromise was reached.

You will find familiar recipes, such as Bubble and Squeak (page 4) and Salmagundy (page 31), old favourites with a new slant, such as Potatoes Stuffed and Baked (page 12) and the classic Russian Salad (pictured below, recipe page 30),

and also 'new' tastes, such as Broccoli with Black Olives (page 2) and Korean Vegetable Salad (page 25). Plus lots of exciting dressings to cheer up the dullest salads, including a fail-safe method of making your own mayonnaise.

Most of our recipes are not only simple and quick to make, they are inexpensive too. But of course there are times (birthdays, anniversaries and so on) when the unusual and the slightly more expensive are desired and we have therefore selected some extra-special dishes **For Special Occasions.** All are guaranteed fit for a king.

There is no healthier way to live than to eat lots of vegetables and salads — and just because they're good for you doesn't mean they have to be dull and uninspired.

Asparagus with Butter Sauce

As well as making a simple but elegant hors d'oeuvre, asparagus is a delicious vegetable accompaniment to meat and fish dishes. The season for fresh asparagus is a short one so frozen asparagus may be used instead.

4 SERVINGS

2 pints [5 cups] water
1 tablespoon plus ¼ teaspoon salt
1 lb. frozen asparagus, thawed and drained
6 tablespoons hot, melted butter
¼ teaspoon freshly ground black pepper

Pour the water into a large saucepan and add 1 tablespoon of the salt. Place the pan over moderate heat and bring the water to the boil. Drop the asparagus into the water. When the water returns to the boil, boil rapidly for 4 to 6 minutes, or until the asparagus is almost tender but still firm.

If the asparagus is not to be served immediately, put in a colander and run cold water through it to prevent it from cooking further and to retain the colour and texture.

Just before serving, put the asparagus in a warmed serving dish and pour the butter over it. Taking care not to break the asparagus, gently toss it in the hot butter to finish the cooking and to coat it with butter. Sprinkle with the remaining salt and the black pepper, and serve at once.

Broccoli with Black Olives

Try this unusual way of serving broccoli — with black olives, garlic and Parmesan cheese. Green olives may be used instead of black, but the colour of the dish will not be as interesting. Serve Broccoli with Black Olives as an accompaniment to grilled [broiled] steaks or pork chops.

4 SERVINGS

1½ lb. broccoli
10 fl. oz. [1¼ cups] water
2 teaspoons salt
3 tablespoons olive oil
1 garlic clove, finely chopped
½ teaspoon freshly ground black pepper
2 oz. [¾ cup] stoned black olives, halved
4 tablespoons finely grated

Parmesan cheese

Wash the broccoli, remove the leaves and break the flowerets into fairly large bunches.

In a large saucepan, bring the water to the boil. Add 1 teaspoon of salt and the broccoli. Cover the pan and cook the broccoli for 10 minutes over moderately high heat. Drain the broccoli. Reserve the water in which the broccoli was cooked.

In a large frying-pan, heat the oil over low heat. Add the garlic and fry for 2 minutes. Add the broccoli and season with the remaining salt and the pepper. Cook the broccoli for 10 minutes, stirring frequently. Add some of the water in which the broccoli was cooked if the pan gets too dry.

Add the olives to the pan and cook for another 2 minutes. Turn the broccoli and olives into a warmed serving dish. Sprinkle with the Parmesan cheese and serve at once.

Asparagus with Butter Sauce is simple enough to be served to the family, elegant enough for a special dinner party.

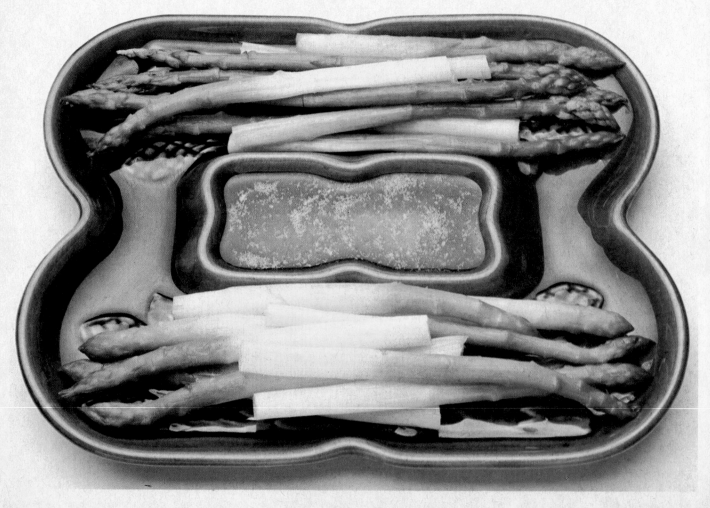

Brussels Sprouts with Chestnuts

An interesting vegetable dish, Brussels Sprouts with Chestnuts goes well with roast chicken, turkey, goose or duck. In this recipe the Brussels sprouts are blanched, plunged in cold water and drained to prevent them from losing their flavour and colour.

6 SERVINGS

1½ lb. fresh or frozen Brussels
    sprouts
2 teaspoons salt
24 chestnuts
2 tablespoons arrowroot
1 tablespoon port or water
15 fl. oz. [1⅞ cups] home-made beef
    stock
2 oz. [¼ cup] butter
½ teaspoon freshly ground black
    pepper
2 oz. [¼ cup] butter, melted

Preheat the oven to warm 325°F (Gas Mark 3, 170°C).

With a sharp knife, trim the base of each Brussels sprout and cut a cross in it. Wash and drain the sprouts, and remove any yellow or wilted leaves.

Fill a large saucepan with water and add 1 teaspoon of salt. Set the pan over moderately high heat and bring the water to the boil. When the water is boiling, drop in the Brussels sprouts and bring the water back to the boil.

Reduce the heat to moderately low and simmer the sprouts slowly for 6 to 8 minutes, or until they are almost tender. Drain off the water and place the saucepan full of sprouts under cold, running water for 3 minutes. Drain the sprouts again

Broccoli with Black Olives makes an unusual vegetable for the family. Serve with steaks or chops.

and place to one side.

Using a sharp knife, split the skins of the chestnuts at the pointed end. Put the chestnuts in a medium-sized saucepan, cover with water and bring them to the boil over moderate heat. Boil for 30 seconds, then drain and peel the chestnuts with a sharp knife.

Put the peeled chestnuts in a large flameproof casserole or baking dish. In a small bowl, mix the arrowroot with the port or water. Then pour in the stock and mix well. Pour this liquid over the chestnuts. Add 1½ ounces [3 tablespoons] of butter. The chestnuts should be well covered with the liquid. If there is not enough liquid to cover, add a little more water.

Place the casserole over moderate heat and bring to the boil. Then cover the casserole and place it in the lower part of the oven. Cook for 45 to 60 minutes or until the chestnuts are tender. (Test them for tenderness by piercing with a sharp pointed knife.)

Take the casserole out of the oven and raise the heat to moderate 350°F (Gas Mark 4, 180°C). Lift the chestnuts out of the casserole with a slotted spoon and discard the cooking liquid. Replace the chestnuts in the casserole and add the Brussels sprouts. Sprinkle with the remaining salt, the black pepper and the melted butter.

With the remaining butter, grease a sheet of greaseproof or waxed paper and carefully cover the casserole with it. Bake in the oven for a further 20 minutes, then

turn the vegetables into a warmed serving dish.

Serve immediately.

Brussels Sprouts Creole

This simple recipe makes a colourful change from plain, boiled Brussels sprouts. It may be served with any savoury dish from an omelet to the Sunday roast.

4 SERVINGS

1½ lb. fresh or frozen Brussels
    sprouts
1½ oz. [3 tablespoons] butter
1 large onion, finely chopped
1 garlic clove, crushed
1 green pepper, white pith removed,
    seeded and chopped
1 lb. tomatoes, blanched, peeled
    and chopped
½ teaspoon freshly ground black
    pepper
¼ teaspoon dried basil
1 teaspoon salt

With a sharp knife, trim any tough or discoloured outer leaves from the sprouts, and wash them thoroughly. Cut a cross in the base of each sprout.

In a heavy, medium-sized saucepan, melt the butter over moderate heat. Add the onion, garlic and green pepper. Cook them, stirring occasionally, for 8 minutes. Add the tomatoes, sprouts, black pepper, basil and salt. Taste the mixture and add more salt and pepper if necessary.

Reduce the heat to low, cover the pan and cook for 15 to 20 minutes, or until the sprouts are tender. Turn the mixture into a warmed serving dish.

Serve at once.

Put the carrot slices into a medium-sized saucepan. Add enough water just to cover the carrots and bring it to the boil over moderate heat. Cover the pan and cook the carrots for 15 minutes, or until they are firm but tender when pierced with a skewer. Using a slotted spoon, remove the carrots from the pan and transfer them to a bowl. Reserve 5 fluid ounces [⅝ cup] of the cooking liquid.

In a medium-sized saucepan, mix together the oil, salt, pepper, cinnamon, cumin seeds, garlic and thyme over very low heat. Simmer for 10 minutes. Add the reserved cooking liquid and the bay leaf, cover the pan and simmer for a further 15 to 20 minutes.

Add the carrots to the saucepan. Toss them in the sauce and cook for 2 to 3 minutes to heat the carrots thoroughly. Sprinkle over the lemon juice, remove the bay leaf and serve immediately, if the dish is to be eaten hot.

Bubble and Squeak

This traditional English dish was originally made from leftover boiled beef, mixed with cold mashed potatoes and greens and then fried. Its name comes from the noise it makes when frying. Today, however, the meat is usually omitted and Bubble and Squeak consists only of leftover mashed potatoes and cabbage. The quantities of each should be approximately equal, but it really depends on how much you have left over.

4 SERVINGS

8 oz. cold mashed potatoes
8 oz. cooked cold cabbage
½ teaspoon salt
¼ teaspoon black pepper
2 oz. [¼ cup] butter
1 teaspoon vinegar

In a large mixing bowl, mix the potatoes and cabbage together. Season with the salt and pepper.

In a large, deep frying-pan, melt the butter over moderately high heat. Add the potato-and-cabbage mixture. Cook for 5 to 6 minutes, or until the potato and cabbage mixture is thoroughly hot, stirring frequently.

Sprinkle the vinegar on top of the mixture. Remove the pan from the heat and turn the Bubble and Squeak into a warmed serving dish. Serve at once.

Cabbage in Sour Cream

Quick and easy to prepare, Cabbage in Sour Cream goes well with lamb dishes.

6 SERVINGS

3 oz. [⅜ cup] butter
1 small green cabbage, coarse outer leaves removed, washed and finely sliced
1 egg, lightly beaten
8 fl. oz. [1 cup] sour cream
2 tablespoons sugar
1 tablespoon white wine vinegar
2 teaspoons caraway seeds
½ teaspoon salt
¼ teaspoon black pepper

In a large saucepan, melt the butter over moderate heat. Add the cabbage and cook for 10 minutes, or until the cabbage is tender but not coloured. Stir occasionally to prevent the cabbage sticking to the pan.

In a medium-sized mixing bowl, combine the egg, sour cream, sugar, vinegar, caraway seeds, salt and pepper. Pour the mixture into the saucepan and stir to coat the cabbage completely with the sauce. Cook for 2 to 3 minutes, stirring constantly. Do not allow the sauce to boil. Transfer it to a warmed serving dish and serve immediately.

Carrots Algerian-Style

Carrots Algerian-Style is equally delicious hot or cold. Serve with boiled beef, roasted pork or lamb.

4 SERVINGS

2 lb. carrots, scraped and cut into ½-inch slices
5 tablespoons olive oil
1 teaspoon salt
½ teaspoon white pepper
½ teaspoon ground cinnamon
½ teaspoon cumin seeds
3 garlic cloves, crushed
½ teaspoon dried thyme
1 bay leaf
1 teaspoon lemon juice

Carrots with Mushrooms

A delicious way of serving carrots, Carrots with Mushrooms is excellent with grilled [broiled] steak or fish.

4 SERVINGS

1 lb. carrots, scraped and sliced
½ teaspoon salt
10 fl. oz. [1¼ cups] water
1 tablespoon sugar
2 oz. [¼ cup] butter
4 oz. mushrooms, wiped clean and quartered
1 tablespoon finely chopped onion

In a medium-sized saucepan, place the carrots, salt, water, sugar and half of the butter over moderate heat. Bring the water to the boil and cover the pan. Reduce the heat to low and simmer the carrots for about 30 minutes, or until they are tender and most of the liquid has been absorbed.

While the carrots are cooking, prepare the mushrooms.

In a small frying-pan, melt the remaining butter over moderate heat. Add the mushrooms and fry them gently for about 3 minutes, or until they are softened. Mix in the onion with a wooden spoon and cook gently for another 3 to 4 minutes.

Add the mushroom mixture to the carrots. Taste and add more salt and pepper if necessary. Turn into a hot serving dish and serve immediately.

Spicy Cauliflower

An exotic dish of cauliflower flavoured with mustard seed, Spicy Cauliflower may be served as part of an Indian meal.

4 SERVINGS

3 tablespoons vegetable oil
1 teaspoon mustard seed
1-inch piece fresh root ginger, peeled and cut into strips
1 onion, sliced
1 teaspoon turmeric
1 green chilli, chopped
1 large cauliflower, trimmed, washed and separated into flowerets
1 teaspoon salt
juice of $\frac{1}{2}$ lemon
3 tablespoons water
1 tablespoon finely chopped fresh coriander leaves

In a large saucepan, heat the oil over moderately high heat. Add the mustard seed, reduce the heat to moderate and cover the pan. When the seeds stop spattering, remove the lid and add the ginger, onion, turmeric and green chilli. Fry, stirring occasionally, for 3 minutes.

Add the cauliflower and salt and stir well. Sprinkle over the lemon juice and water, cover the pan, reduce the heat to low and cook the cauliflower for 20 minutes, or until the flowerets are tender.

Turn the contents of the pan into a warmed serving dish. Sprinkle over the chopped coriander leaves and serve.

Cauliflower with Tomatoes and Cheese

An elegant dish requiring minimal preparation, Cauliflower with Tomatoes and Cheese may be served with chops or omelets.

4-6 SERVINGS

1 tablespoon butter
1 large cauliflower, trimmed, washed and separated into flowerets
6 tomatoes, blanched, peeled, seeded and roughly chopped

Cauliflower with Tomatoes and Cheese is a hearty dish, absolutely guaranteed to satisfy the hungriest family!

$\frac{1}{2}$ teaspoon salt
$\frac{1}{4}$ teaspoon black pepper
4 oz. [$\frac{1}{2}$ cup] butter, melted
2 tablespoons dry breadcrumbs
2 tablespoons grated Parmesan cheese
2 tablespoons grated Emmenthal cheese

Preheat the oven to fairly hot 375°F (Gas Mark 5, 190°C).

Lightly grease a large shallow casserole with the tablespoon of butter.

In a large saucepan, cook the cauliflower flowerets in boiling salted water over moderate heat for 9 to 12 minutes, or until they are tender. Drain the flowerets.

Place the flowerets in the buttered casserole. Arrange the chopped tomatoes on top and sprinkle with salt, pepper and half of the melted butter.

In a small bowl, combine the breadcrumbs with the Parmesan and Emmenthal cheeses and sprinkle the mixture over the vegetable pieces. Spoon the remaining melted butter over the mixture and bake in the oven for about 30 minutes, or until the top is golden brown. Remove the dish from the oven and serve immediately.

Grilled Courgettes [Broiled Zucchini]

Grilled Courgettes [Broiled Zucchini] makes an unusual accompaniment to grilled [broiled] chops, roasts or steaks, or it may be served on its own as a light luncheon or supper dish. If you serve it on its own, accompany it with lots of crusty bread, a baked potato and, to drink, some well-chilled white wine.

4 SERVINGS

1 tablespoon butter
8 courgettes [zucchini], trimmed, cleaned and blanched
2 garlic cloves, crushed
2 teaspoons sugar
1 teaspoon salt
1 tablespoon chopped fresh dill or 1½ teaspoons dried dill
1 medium-sized onion, sliced and pushed out into rings
3 oz. [¾ cup] Parmesan cheese, grated

Preheat the oven to moderate 350°F (Gas Mark 4, 180°C). Grease a shallow flame-proof baking dish with the tablespoon of butter.

With a sharp knife, slice the courgettes [zucchini] in half, lengthways, and arrange them in the bottom of the baking dish, skin side down. Sprinkle them with the

Serve Courgettes [Zucchini] Provençal-Style as a delicious accompaniment to omelets or chops.

garlic, sugar, salt and dill and arrange the onion rings over the top. Spread the grated cheese on top of the mixture and bake in the upper part of the oven for 15 minutes.

Preheat the grill [broiler] to moderately high.

Remove the courgettes [zucchini] from the oven and place them under the grill [broiler] for 4 minutes, or until the cheese is bubbly and brown.

Serve immediately.

Courgettes [Zucchini] Provençal-Style

A delicious vegetable dish, Courgettes [Zucchini] Provençal-Style is a must for garlic lovers. Serve it with grilled [broiled] steak or omelets, or by itself with crusty bread for a light but sustaining luncheon dish.

4 SERVINGS

8 courgettes [zucchini], trimmed, cleaned and blanched
4 tablespoons olive oil
½ teaspoon salt

½ teaspoon freshly ground black pepper
3 garlic cloves, crushed
2 oz. [⅔ cup] fine dry breadcrumbs
2 tablespoons finely chopped fresh parsley

Cut the courgettes [zucchini] into ½-inch slices, crosswise, and dry them thoroughly on kitchen paper towels.

In a large frying-pan, heat the olive oil over moderate heat. When the oil is hot, add the courgettes [zucchini] to the pan and cook them for 8 to 10 minutes, stirring occasionally with a wooden spoon to prevent them from sticking to the bottom of the pan.

Raise the heat to fairly high and stir in the salt, pepper, garlic, breadcrumbs and parsley. Remove the pan from the heat and toss the ingredients gently together until they are well mixed. Transfer the mixture to a warmed serving dish and serve immediately.

French Beans, Hungarian-Style

A colourful and unusual vegetable dish, French Beans, Hungarian-Style goes particularly well with grilled [broiled] pork or lamb chops or steaks or fried or grilled

[broiled] *fish*.

1½ pints [3¾ cups] water
1 teaspoon salt
1 lb. French beans, trimmed and washed
2 tablespoons vegetable oil or olive oil
2 medium-sized onions, finely chopped
1 tablespoon paprika
1 tablespoon tomato purée
5 fl. oz. [⅝ cup] sour cream

In a large saucepan, bring the water to the boil over high heat. Add the salt and the French beans to the pan. Reduce the heat to moderately low and simmer the beans for 5 to 15 minutes, or until they are just tender.

Remove the pan from the heat and drain the beans in a large colander. Set aside.

In a large frying-pan, heat the oil over moderate heat. When the oil is hot, add the onions to the pan. Fry them, stirring occasionally, for 5 to 7 minutes, or until they are soft and translucent but not brown.

Remove the pan from the heat. With a wooden spoon, stir the paprika, tomato purée and sour cream into the onion mixture.

Return the pan to low heat and mix in the drained beans. Cook, stirring occasionally, for 5 minutes or until the beans and sauce are heated through.

Remove the pan from the heat and turn the mixture into a large, warmed serving dish.

Serve at once.

French Beans with Apples and Almonds

An unusual accompaniment, French Beans with Apples and Almonds goes marvellously well with venison, grilled [broiled] or fried beef steaks, or any of the other darker meats, such as hare.

1½ pints [3¾ cups] water
1 teaspoon salt
1 lb. French beans, trimmed, washed and halved
3 oz. [⅜ cup] butter

A tasty way of cooking a delicious vegetable, French Beans, Hungarian-Style combines beans, onions, paprika and sour cream.

1 medium-sized onion, very thinly sliced and pushed out into rings
2 medium-sized cooking apples, peeled, cored and very roughly chopped
1 oz. [¼ cup] flaked blanched almonds

In a large saucepan, bring the water to the boil over high heat. Add the salt and French beans to the pan. Reduce the heat to moderately low and simmer the beans for 5 to 15 minutes, or until they are just tender.

Remove the pan from the heat and drain the beans in a large colander. Set the beans aside.

In a large frying-pan, melt the butter over moderate heat. When the foam subsides, add the onion and apples to the pan. Cook them, stirring occasionally, for 8 to 10 minutes, or until the onion is golden brown and the apples are tender but still firm.

Stir in the beans and almonds and reduce the heat to low. Cook the mixture, stirring frequently, for 5 minutes or until the beans are heated through.

Remove the pan from the heat and transfer the mixture to a warmed serving dish.

Serve at once.

Lettuces Baked with Shrimps

Lettuces Baked with Shrimps can either be served as a light lunch or, baked in individual ramekin dishes (as pictured below), as a first course to an informal lunch or dinner.

4 SERVINGS

8 fl. oz. double cream [1 cup heavy cream]

2 teaspoons prepared French mustard

1 teaspoon Worcestershire sauce

$\frac{1}{8}$ teaspoon cayenne pepper

$\frac{1}{8}$ teaspoon grated nutmeg

$\frac{1}{2}$ teaspoon salt

$\frac{1}{4}$ teaspoon freshly ground black pepper

$\frac{1}{4}$ teaspoon Tabasco sauce

1 teaspoon cornflour [cornstarch] dissolved in 1 tablespoon double [heavy] cream

2 medium-sized lettuces, coarse outer leaves removed, washed, shaken dry and very finely shredded

1 tablespoon butter

8 oz. frozen and thawed shrimps, shelled

4 medium-sized tomatoes, blanched, peeled, seeded and chopped

2 teaspoons lemon juice

2 oz. [$\frac{1}{2}$ cup] Parmesan cheese, grated

Preheat the oven to fairly hot 375°F (Gas Mark 5, 190°C).

In a medium-sized saucepan, combine the cream, mustard, Worcestershire sauce, cayenne pepper, nutmeg, salt, black pepper, Tabasco sauce and the cornflour [cornstarch] mixture. Set the saucepan over moderately low heat and cook the sauce for 3 to 4 minutes, or until it is thick and smooth. Remove the pan from the heat and stir in the shredded lettuces. Stir well to coat them thoroughly. Set the mixture aside.

Using the tablespoon of butter, generously grease a large baking dish. Spread half the lettuce mixture in the bottom of the dish. Cover with the shrimps and cover the shrimps with the chopped tomatoes.

Spread the remaining lettuce mixture over the tomatoes. Sprinkle over the lemon juice and cover with the grated Parmesan cheese.

Place the dish in the centre of the oven and bake for 35 to 40 minutes, or until the lettuce is tender and the top lightly browned.

Remove the dish from the oven and serve the mixture immediately, straight from the dish.

Marrow [Summer Squash] with Savoury Stuffing

An inexpensive dish, Marrow [Summer Squash] with Savoury Stuffing makes the ideal winter family meal. Serve with mashed potatoes, hot tomato sauce and lots of sautéed or steamed French beans.

6 SERVINGS

2 oz. [$\frac{1}{4}$ cup] plus 1 tablespoon butter

1 x 3 lb. vegetable marrow [summer squash]

2 medium-sized onions, coarsely chopped

1 large green pepper, white pith removed, seeded and coarsely

Lettuces Baked with Shrimps—a delightfully different and elegant dish to serve for a light family supper or lunch.

Serve Marrow [Summer Squash] with Savoury Stuffing as an inexpensive but filling lunch or supper, guaranteed to satisfy the whole family.

chopped
1 lb. lean beef, finely minced [ground]
4 medium-sized tomatoes, blanched, peeled, seeded and coarsely chopped
2 small carrots, scraped, cooked and diced
1½ teaspoons salt
½ teaspoon freshly ground black pepper
1 teaspoon paprika
1 teaspoon chopped fresh thyme or ½ teaspoon dried thyme
2 oz. [1 cup] fresh white breadcrumbs
2 medium-sized egg yolks, well beaten with 2 fl. oz. single cream [¼ cup light cream]
4 oz. [1 cup] Parmesan cheese, finely grated

Preheat the oven to moderate 350°F (Gas Mark 4, 180°C).

With the tablespoon of butter, generously grease a large, oblong baking dish and set it aside.

With a long, sharp knife (a bread knife is ideal), cut the marrow [summer squash] in half, lengthways. With a sharp-edged metal spoon, scoop out and discard the seeds, making a cavity in the centre of each marrow [summer squash] half. Place the marrow [summer squash] halves, side by side and with the cut sides upwards, in the prepared baking dish and set aside.

In a medium-sized saucepan, melt 1 ounce [2 tablespoons] of the remaining butter over moderate heat. When the foam subsides, add the onions and green pepper and fry, stirring occasionally, for 8 to 10 minutes, or until the onions are golden brown and the green pepper is translucent.

Add the minced [ground] beef and tomatoes to the pan and cook, stirring and turning occasionally to break up the meat, for 6 to 8 minutes, or until it loses its pinkness.

Remove the pan from the heat. Stir in the diced carrots, salt, black pepper, paprika and fresh or dried thyme. Set the mixture aside.

In a small mixing bowl, combine the breadcrumbs with the egg yolks and cream mixture. Stir the mixture into the meat mixture in the saucepan and beat briskly to combine the stuffing as thoroughly as possible.

Pile the stuffing into the cavities of the marrow [summer squash] halves. Lightly pat the stuffing down with the back of a wooden spoon so that the centres are domed slightly.

Sprinkle the Parmesan cheese over the stuffing. Cut the remaining butter into small pieces and dot them over the cheese. Place the dish in the centre of the oven and bake for 1 to 1¼ hours or until the marrow [summer squash] is very tender when pierced with the point of a sharp knife, and the filling is cooked and well browned.

Remove the marrow [summer squash] from the oven and transfer the halves to a deep, warmed serving dish.

Serve at once.

Stuffed Mushrooms

These mushrooms, filled with a cream and parsley mixture and topped with cheese, are delicious and easy to prepare. They may be served either as an appetizing hors d'oeuvre, as an attractive garnish to a roast or as a simple, after-school snack for hungry children.

4 SERVINGS

12 large mushrooms, wiped clean
1 teaspoon salt
½ teaspoon freshly ground black pepper
1 teaspoon melted butter
1 oz. [2 tablespoons] butter
2 shallots or spring onions [scallions], finely chopped
1 tablespoon flour
4 fl. oz. single cream [½ cup light cream]
3 tablespoons finely chopped fresh parsley
1½ tablespoons grated Parmesan cheese

Preheat the oven to fairly hot 375°F (Gas Mark 5, 190°C).

Remove the stems from the mushrooms and set them aside. Season the mushroom caps with ½ teaspoon of the salt and ¼ teaspoon of the black pepper and, using a pastry brush, coat them with the melted butter. Arrange them, hollow side up, in a lightly greased shallow baking dish. Set the dish aside while you prepare the stuffing.

With a sharp knife, chop the mushroom stems finely. Wrap them in kitchen paper towels and twist the towels to extract as much juice from the mushroom stems as possible.

In a medium-sized frying-pan, melt the 1 ounce [2 tablespoons] of butter over moderate heat.

When the foam subsides, add the chopped mushroom stems and shallots or spring onions [scallions]. Sauté them together for 3 to 4 minutes, or until the shallots or spring onions [scallions] are soft and translucent but not brown. Reduce the heat to low and, stirring constantly, add the flour to the pan. Cook for 1 minute.

Remove the pan from the heat and stir in the cream, a little at a time. When the sauce is smooth and all the ingredients are thoroughly blended, return the pan to the heat and simmer the sauce for 2 to 3 minutes, or until it has thickened and is smooth.

Stir in the parsley and the remaining salt and pepper and mix well.

Remove the pan from the heat and spoon a little of the mixture into each of the prepared mushroom caps.

Top each mushroom with a little grated cheese. Place the dish in the oven and bake the mushrooms for 15 minutes or until they are tender and the stuffing is lightly browned on top.

Remove from the oven and serve.

Onion Pie

This Onion Pie makes a perfect main course for a vegetarian meal or it may be served as a first course. Serve either hot or cold, with a tossed green salad, lots of crusty bread and, to drink, some well-chilled lager or cider.

4-6 SERVINGS

1 x 9-inch flan case, made with frozen and thawed shortcrust pastry, baked blind
1 oz. [2 tablespoons] butter
4 medium-sized onions, thinly sliced
5 spring onions [scallions], finely chopped
2 eggs, lightly beaten
6 fl. oz. single cream [¾ cup light cream]
4 oz. [1 cup] Cheddar cheese, finely grated
1 tablespoon chopped fresh basil or 1½ teaspoons dried basil
1 tablespoon finely chopped fresh parsley
1 teaspoon salt
½ teaspoon freshly ground black pepper

Preheat the oven to fairly hot 375°F (Gas Mark 5, 190°C).

Place the flan case on a large baking sheet. Set aside.

In a large frying-pan, melt the butter over moderate heat. When the foam subsides, add the onions and spring onions [scallions]. Cook, stirring occasionally, for 5 to 7 minutes, or until all of the onions are soft and translucent but not brown.

Remove the pan from the heat and set aside.

In a medium-sized mixing bowl, lightly beat the eggs, cream and cheese together with a fork. Stir in the basil, parsley, salt and pepper. Add the onion mixture and mix well.

Pour the mixture into the flan case and place the baking sheet in the centre of the oven. Bake the pie for 35 to 40 minutes, or until the filling has risen and the top is lightly browned.

Remove the baking sheet from the oven. Serve immediately, or allow to cool before serving.

Small Garden Peas with Bacon and Onions

Small Garden Peas with Bacon and Onions is a classic French way of preparing garden peas. Serve with grilled [broiled] steaks, roast beef or roast lamb.

4-6 SERVINGS

4 streaky bacon slices, rinds removed and diced
1 tablespoon butter
5 small white onions, peeled and finely chopped
2 tablespoons flour
½ teaspoon salt

½ teaspoon freshly ground black
  pepper
8 fl. oz. [1 cup] veal or chicken
  stock
  bouquet garni, consisting of 4
  parsley sprigs, 1 thyme spray
  and 1 bay leaf tied together
1½ lb. small fresh garden peas,
  weighed after shelling or 1½ lb.
  frozen petits pois, thawed

In a medium-sized saucepan, fry the bacon over moderately high heat, stirring occasionally, for 6 to 8 minutes or until it is crisp and has rendered most of its fat.

With a slotted spoon, remove the bacon from the pan and set it aside to drain on kitchen paper towels.

Reduce the heat to moderate and add the butter to the pan. When the foam subsides, add the onions and fry them, stirring occasionally, for 8 to 10 minutes or until they are golden brown.

Remove the pan from the heat. With a slotted spoon, remove the onions from the pan and add them to the bacon. Using a wooden spoon, stir in the flour, salt and pepper into the pan to make a smooth paste. Gradually add the stock, stirring constantly and being careful to avoid lumps. Add the bouquet garni and the reserved onions and bacon. Return the pan to the heat.

Bring the liquid to the boil, stirring constantly. Stir in the peas and reduce the heat to low. Cover the pan and simmer for 6 to 8 minutes, stirring occasionally, or until the peas are tender.

Remove the pan from the heat and remove and discard the bouquet garni. Spoon the mixture into a warmed serving dish.

Serve immediately.

Delightful Small Garden Peas with Bacon and Onions are a very special family treat.

A classic dish, Potatoes Dauphinoise complements roast lamb or beef quite beautifully.

with oil. Heat the oil in one pan over moderate heat until it reaches 325°F on a deep-fat thermometer or until a piece of stale bread dropped into the oil turns golden brown in 65 seconds.

Heat the oil in the other pan over moderate heat until it reaches 375°F on a deep-fat thermometer or until a piece of stale bread dropped into the oil turns golden brown in 40 seconds.

Drop the potato slices into the first pan and fry them for 4 minutes.

Using a slotted spoon, transfer the slices to the second pan and fry them for 2 to 3 minutes or until they puff up. Immediately the slices puff up, remove them from the oil and drain them on kitchen paper towels.

Sprinkle with the salt and serve.

Potatoes Stuffed and Baked

Baked potatoes are doubly delicious when the flesh is scooped out, mixed with savoury ingredients, returned to the shell and reheated in the oven until the top is golden.

First bake the potatoes in their jackets, remove them from the oven and place them on a board. Remove a ½-inch slice from the top flat side of the potato. Scoop out the inside of each potato to within ¼-inch of the shell, being careful not to pierce the skin. Place the flesh in a mixing bowl and arrange the shells in a roasting tin. Prepare the filling and spoon it into the potato shells, piling it up and rounding the top. Place the potatoes in an oven preheated to fairly hot 375°F (Gas Mark 5, 190°C) and bake them for 10 to 12 minutes or until the top of the filling is golden brown.

FILLING 1
   the flesh from 4 potatoes baked
   in their jackets
2 oz. Brie cheese
½ teaspoon dried chives
½ teaspoon salt
1 egg yolk
2 oz. [¼ cup] butter, softened

In a medium-sized mixing bowl, combine the potato flesh, Brie, chives, salt, egg yolk and butter. Beat them with a wooden spoon until they are all thoroughly mixed.

FILLING 2
   the flesh from 4 potatoes baked
   in their jackets
2 oz. Gorgonzola cheese, crumbled
1 tablespoon single [light] cream

Potatoes Dauphinoise

One of the classic French potato dishes, Potatoes Dauphinoise goes magnificently with roast lamb.

6 SERVINGS
1 garlic clove, halved
1 oz. [2 tablespoons] butter
2 lb. potatoes, peeled and cut into
   ¼-inch slices
1 teaspoon salt
1 teaspoon black pepper
6 oz. [1½ cups] Cheddar cheese,
   grated
1 egg, lightly beaten
10 fl. oz. [1¼ cups] milk, scalded
⅛ teaspoon grated nutmeg

Preheat the oven to fairly hot 375°F (Gas Mark 5, 190°C).

Rub the garlic over the bottom and sides of a medium-sized baking dish. Grease the dish with half the butter.

Place about one-third of the potato slices in the baking dish and sprinkle over ½ teaspoon of the salt, ½ teaspoon of the pepper and 1 ounce [¼ cup] of the grated cheese. Top with another one-third of the potatoes. Sprinkle on the remaining salt and pepper and a further 1 ounce [¼ cup] of cheese and top with the remaining potato slices.

In a small saucepan, beat the egg, milk and nutmeg together with a fork until they are well blended. Place the pan over moderate heat and bring to the boil. Remove the pan from the heat and pour the mixture into the baking dish.

Sprinkle the remaining grated cheese over the top. Cut the remaining butter into small pieces and dot them on top.

Place the dish in the oven and bake for 45 to 50 minutes, or until the potatoes are tender but still firm.

Remove from the oven and serve.

Potato Puffs

Potato Puffs are thinly sliced potatoes fried in two lots of oil — the first at a low temperature, the second at a high temperature. This method of frying makes the potatoes puff up. Serve with grilled [broiled] meat or fish.

2-4 SERVINGS
1 lb. potatoes, peeled and cut into
   ⅛-inch thick slices
   sufficient vegetable oil for
   deep-frying
1 teaspoon salt

Place the potato slices in a large bowl of cold water for 30 minutes. Drain them and dry thoroughly with a clean cloth.

Fill two large saucepans one-third full

2 teaspoons tomato purée
½ teaspoon black pepper
½ teaspoon dried basil
2 oz. [¼ cup] butter, softened

In a medium-sized mixing bowl, combine the potato flesh, Gorgonzola, cream, tomato purée, pepper, basil and butter. Beat them with a wooden spoon until they are thoroughly mixed.

FILLING 3
    the flesh from 4 potatoes baked
    in their jackets
4 oz. Cheshire cheese, crumbled
1 small eating apple, peeled, cored
    and finely chopped
1 teaspoon prepared mustard
½ teaspoon salt
2 oz. [¼ cup] butter, softened

Potatoes Stuffed and Baked six ways to make marvellous snacks for hungry children and fabulous accompaniments to meat dishes.

In a medium-sized mixing bowl, combine the potato flesh, Cheshire, apple, mustard, salt and butter. Beat them with a wooden spoon until they are thoroughly mixed.

FILLING 4
    the flesh from 4 potatoes baked
    in their jackets
4 oz. [1 cup] Cheddar cheese, grated
2 teaspoons sour-sweet chutney
1 small celery stalk, finely chopped
2 oz. [¼ cup] butter, softened

In a medium-sized mixing bowl, combine the potato flesh, Cheddar, chutney, celery and butter. Beat them with a wooden spoon until they are thoroughly mixed.

FILLING 5
    the flesh from 4 potatoes baked
    in their jackets
4 slices bacon, grilled [broiled]
    until golden and crumbled
1 oz. [2 tablespoons] butter
4 oz. mushrooms, chopped
½ teaspoon salt
¼ teaspoon black pepper

In a medium-sized mixing bowl, combine the potato flesh and the bacon. Set aside.

In a small frying-pan, melt the butter over moderate heat. When the foam subsides, add the mushrooms and fry, stirring constantly, for 3 minutes. Remove the pan from the heat and pour the contents of the pan into the mixing bowl. Add the salt and pepper. Beat the ingredients with a wooden spoon until they are mixed.

FILLING 6
    the flesh from 4 potatoes baked
    in their jackets
4 oz. shrimps, shelled
4 spring onions [scallions], chopped
½ teaspoon grated lemon rind
½ teaspoon chopped fresh parsley
¼ teaspoon cayenne pepper
2 oz. [¼ cup] butter, softened

In a medium-sized mixing bowl, combine the potato flesh, shrimps, spring onions [scallions], lemon rind, parsley, cayenne and butter. Beat with a wooden spoon until they are thoroughly mixed.

13

Creamed Spinach

This rich, smooth vegetable dish goes beautifully with baked ham, liver, sweet-breads, chicken or veal. It may be garnished with two chopped hard-boiled eggs.

4 SERVINGS

4 pints [5 pints] water
2 teaspoons salt
2 lb. frozen and thawed
   spinach, washed and chopped
1 tablespoon butter
1 tablespoon flour
10 fl. oz. single cream [1¼ cups light
   cream]
¼ teaspoon black pepper

In a large saucepan, bring the water and salt to the boil over high heat. Add the spinach and when the water boils again reduce the heat to moderate and cook gently for 10 minutes, or until the spinach is tender.

Drain off the liquid leaving the spinach in the saucepan.

In a small heavy saucepan, melt the butter over low heat. Remove the pan from the heat and, with a wooden spoon, stir in the flour. Gradually add the cream, stirring constantly. Return the pan to moderate heat and bring the sauce to the boil. Stirring constantly, cook for 5 minutes. Add the pepper.

Pour the sauce over the spinach in the large saucepan and return to moderate heat. Stir to mix. Cook for 2 minutes to reheat the spinach and remove the pan from the heat. Serve at once.

Spinach with Cheese

An excellent and simple-to-make vegetable dish, Spinach with Cheese makes a delicious accompaniment to cold meats.

4 SERVINGS

2 lb. frozen and thawed spinach,
   washed and chopped
1½ teaspoons salt
4 oz. [½ cup] butter
4 oz. [1 cup] Cheddar cheese,
   finely grated
½ teaspoon black pepper

Put the spinach in a large saucepan. Pour over enough water just to cover the spinach. Add 1 teaspoon of the salt and place the pan over moderately high heat. Bring the water to the boil. Reduce the heat to moderate and cook the spinach for 10 minutes. Drain the spinach in a colander, pressing it well down with a wooden spoon to remove all excess liquid.

In a large frying-pan, melt the butter over moderate heat. When the foam sub-sides, add the spinach to the pan. Gradually stir in three-quarters of the cheese with a wooden spoon and cook, still stirring, for 3 minutes, or until the ingredients are well blended. Add the pepper and remaining salt.

Preheat the grill [broiler] to high.

Remove the pan from the heat and transfer the spinach mixture to a flame-proof casserole. Sprinkle the remaining cheese on top of the spinach and place it under the grill [broiler]. Cook for 7 to 10 minutes, or until the cheese is golden and melted.

Remove the casserole from the heat and serve immediately.

Sweetcorn Moulds

Creamy sweetcorn custards garnished with watercress and crispy bacon make these moulds a really unusual first course.

6 SERVINGS

1 teaspoon vegetable oil
10 oz. canned creamed sweetcorn
4 oz. [1 cup] Gruyère cheese, grated
5 fl. oz. double cream [⅝ cup heavy
   cream]
1 teaspoon salt
½ teaspoon black pepper
2 teaspoons prepared mustard
4 eggs, lightly beaten
GARNISH
2 bunches watercress, washed and
   shaken dry
8 oz. streaky bacon, rinds removed,
   grilled [broiled] **until crisp and**
   crumbled

Preheat the oven to warm 325°F (Gas Mark 3, 170°C).

Using the teaspoon of oil, lightly grease 6 dariole moulds. Set aside.

In a medium-sized mixing bowl, com-bine the sweetcorn, cheese, cream, salt, pepper and mustard, beating well until the ingredients are thoroughly combined. Gradually beat in the eggs. Spoon the mixture into the prepared dariole moulds. Place the moulds in a large roasting tin and pour in enough boiling water to come half way up the sides of the moulds. Place the tin in the oven and bake for 45 minutes or until a knife inserted into the centre of each mould comes out clean.

Remove the tin from the oven and take out the moulds. Set aside for 5 minutes.

Run a knife around the edge of the moulds to loosen the sides. Hold indi-vidual serving plates, inverted, over each of the moulds and reverse the two. The moulds should slide out easily. Garnish with the watercress and crumbled bacon

and serve at once.

Tomato Pie

An economical supper dish, Tomato Pie is ideal for vegetarians. A green salad and lots of lightly buttered brown bread are all that are needed to accompany this dish.

4-6 SERVINGS

1 teaspoon butter
12 oz. [3 cups] frozen and thawed
   shortcrust pastry
1 lb. firm tomatoes, thinly sliced
1 medium-sized onion, very thinly
   sliced and pushed out into rings
4 oz. button mushrooms, wiped
   clean and coarsely chopped
½ teaspoon salt
½ teaspoon freshly ground black
   pepper
1 teaspoon dried oregano
1 teaspoon dry mustard
4 oz. [1 cup] Cheddar cheese,
   grated
1 egg, lightly beaten

Preheat the oven to fairly hot 400°F (Gas Mark 6, 200°C). With the teaspoon of butter, grease a 9-inch pie plate and set aside.

On a lightly floured board, roll out half the dough to a 10-inch circle. Using the rolling pin, lift the dough on to the plate and press it down with your fingertips. Trim off any excess with a table knife. Reserve the trimmings.

Arrange half the tomatoes, onion and mushrooms in the centre of the plate, leaving the rim clear. Sprinkle over half the salt, pepper, oregano, mustard and cheese. Continue making layers in this way until all the ingredients have been used. Dampen the edges of the dough with water.

Roll out the remaining dough to a 10-inch circle. Using the rolling pin, lift the dough over the filling and press the edges together. Trim off any excess, and reserve it. Crimp the edges together to seal them. Roll out the trimmings, cut them into fancy shapes and use them to decorate the pie. With a pastry brush, brush the dough with the beaten egg. Cut a small cross in the centre of the pie.

Place the plate on a baking sheet and place the baking sheet in the oven. Bake for 20 to 25 minutes or until the pastry is golden brown and crisp.

Remove the baking sheet from the oven and serve the pie at once.

Serve Tomato Pie as a light lunch or supper dish for the family.

Tomatoes Stuffed with Anchovies, Breadcrumbs and Garlic

☆ ☆ ① ✕

These classic stuffed tomatoes are simply delicious as a first course for a dinner party. They may be served either hot or cold.

6 SERVINGS

- 2 tablespoons olive oil
- 10 tomatoes, 6 halved and seeded and 4 peeled, seeded and roughly chopped
- 2 teaspoons finely chopped fresh parsley
- 2 garlic cloves, crushed
- 3 oz. [1½ cups] fresh breadcrumbs, 2 oz. [1 cup] soaked in 2 fl. oz. [¼ cup] home-made beef stock for 10 minutes
- 4 anchovy fillets, very finely chopped
- 2 tablespoons grated Parmesan cheese

Preheat the oven to moderate 350°F (Gas Mark 4, 180°C).

In a medium-sized flameproof casserole, heat half of the oil over moderate heat. When the oil is hot, add the halved tomatoes, cut sides up, and fry for 1 minute. With a slotted spoon, transfer the tomatoes to an ovenproof baking dish and set aside.

Add ½ tablespoon of the remaining oil to the casserole. Add the chopped tomatoes, the parsley and garlic and cover the casserole. Cook, stirring occasionally, for 5 minutes.

Meanwhile, using the back of a wooden spoon, rub the soaked breadcrumbs through a fine wire strainer into a small bowl. Set aside.

Stir the puréed breadcrumbs and the anchovies into the mixture in the casserole and cook for a further 2 minutes, stirring occasionally.

Remove the casserole from the heat and, using a teaspoon, spoon equal quantities of the stuffing mixture into each tomato half.

In a small bowl, mix together the remaining breadcrumbs and the cheese. Sprinkle this mixture over each tomato half and dribble over the remaining oil.

Place the baking dish in the centre of the oven and bake for 15 to 20 minutes. Remove the dish from the oven and serve immediately, straight from the baking dish.

Alternatively, set the baking dish aside and allow the tomatoes to cool completely before serving.

Turnip, Potato and Carrot Hash

 ①

A very economical and tasty dish, Turnip, Potato and Carrot Hash makes an excellent accompaniment to boiled beef or grilled [broiled] sausages.

6 SERVINGS

1 large turnip, peeled and coarsely chopped
3 medium-sized carrots, scraped and coarsely chopped
1 large onion, coarsely chopped
3 medium-sized potatoes, peeled and coarsely chopped
8 fl. oz. [1 cup] canned beef consommé
½ teaspoon salt
1½ teaspoons freshly ground black pepper
1 tablespoon butter, cut into small pieces

Place the turnip, carrots, onion and potatoes in a medium-sized saucepan and add the consommé and salt. Place the saucepan over high heat and bring the liquid to the boil. Reduce the heat to moderately low and simmer the mixture, uncovered, for 20 to 30 minutes or until the vegetables are very tender and most of the liquid has been absorbed.

Preheat the oven to fairly hot 400°F (Gas Mark 6, 200°C).

Remove the pan from the heat and pour off any excess liquid. Add the pepper to the pan and, using a potato masher or fork, mash the vegetables until they form a thick purée.

Transfer the mixture to a medium-sized baking dish, smoothing over the surface with the back of a fork. Dot the surface with the butter.

Place the baking dish in the oven and bake for 10 to 15 minutes or until the top of the mixture is golden brown.

Remove the dish from the oven and serve immediately, straight from the dish.

Vegetable Curry

 ①

This is a simple curry which can be made with almost any combination of vegetables. Serve with boiled rice, chutneys and poppadums.

4-6 SERVINGS

3 tablespoons vegetable oil
2 medium-sized onions, finely chopped
1½-inch piece fresh root ginger, peeled and very finely chopped
2 garlic cloves, crushed
2 green chillis, seeded and finely chopped
1 teaspoon turmeric
1 tablespoon ground coriander
1 tablespoon paprika
½ teaspoon cayenne pepper
¼ teaspoon ground fenugreek
¼ teaspoon freshly ground black pepper
2 tablespoons lemon juice
1 lb. potatoes, peeled and cut into 1-inch cubes
8 oz. turnips, peeled and cut into 1-inch cubes
8 oz. carrots, scraped and cut into ¼-inch slices
4 oz. French beans, trimmed and sliced
4 oz. fresh peas, weighed after shelling
1 teaspoon salt

This colourful and nutritious Vegetable Curry is very easy and quick to make and has an authentically hot Indian taste.

14 oz. canned peeled tomatoes, rubbed through a strainer with the can juice

In a large saucepan, heat the oil over moderate heat. When the oil is hot, add the onions, ginger, garlic and chillis and fry, stirring occasionally, for 8 to 10 minutes or until the onions are golden.

Meanwhile, in a small bowl, combine the turmeric, coriander, paprika, cayenne pepper, fenugreek and pepper. Add the lemon juice and a little water, if necessary, to make a smooth paste. Add the spice paste to the onion mixture and fry, stirring constantly, for 5 minutes. Add a spoonful of water if the mixture gets too dry. Add the vegetables to the pan and fry, stirring constantly, for 5 minutes. Stir in the salt and the strained tomatoes and bring the mixture to the boil. Cover the pan, reduce the heat to low and simmer the curry for 20 to 25 minutes or until the vegetables are cooked. Taste the curry and add more salt if necessary. Remove the pan from the heat.

Transfer the curry to a deep serving dish and serve immediately.

Vegetable Rissoles

Filling and nourishing, Vegetable Rissoles make an ideal vegetarian lunch or supper dish, and the children will love them. Serve with mashed potatoes and brown bread.

4 SERVINGS

4 oz. [½ cup] red lentils, soaked overnight, cooked and drained
1 large onion, finely chopped
1 celery stalk, trimmed and finely chopped
2 small carrots, scraped and grated
2 oz. French beans, cooked and finely chopped
2 oz. [1 cup] fresh white bread-crumbs
3 eggs
1½ teaspoons salt
1 teaspoon freshly ground black pepper
1 teaspoon dried mixed herbs
3 oz. [1 cup] dry white breadcrumbs
2 fl. oz. [¼ cup] vegetable oil

Place the lentils, onion, celery, carrots, beans, fresh white breadcrumbs, 2 of the eggs, the salt and pepper and mixed

Children will love these filling Vegetable Rissoles—and they're good for them too!

herbs in a medium-sized mixing bowl. Using a wooden spoon, mix well until the ingredients are thoroughly combined. Set the mixture aside at room temperature for 30 minutes.

Using your hands, shape the mixture into 8 equal-sized balls and flatten the balls between the palms of your hands to make small cakes. Set aside.

Using a fork, beat the remaining egg in a small shallow dish. Place the dry breadcrumbs on a plate. Dip each rissole first in the egg and then into the breadcrumbs, coating the rissoles thoroughly and shaking off any excess crumbs.

In a medium-sized frying-pan, heat the vegetable oil over moderate heat. When the oil is hot, add the rissoles and fry them for 10 minutes on each side or until they are golden brown.

Remove the pan from the heat. Using a fish slice, transfer the rissoles to kitchen paper towels and drain. Place the rissoles on a warmed serving dish and serve immediately.

Braised Carrots and Bacon

A rich vegetable accompaniment with a difference, Braised Carrots and Bacon is not difficult or expensive to make. It goes well with omelets or grilled [broiled] meats.

2-3 SERVINGS

1 lb. carrots, scraped and cut into
   1-inch slices
1 tablespoon butter
8 oz. lean bacon, coarsely chopped
2 fl. oz. double cream [¼ cup heavy
   cream]
1 teaspoon grated nutmeg
½ teaspoon salt
½ teaspoon black pepper
2 oz. [½ cup] Gruyère cheese, grated
   parsley sprigs (to garnish)

Place the carrot slices in a medium-sized saucepan. Add enough salted water to cover, and bring to the boil over moderate heat. Cook the carrots for 10 minutes. Remove the pan from the heat and drain the carrots thoroughly in a colander.

In a medium-sized frying-pan, melt the butter over moderate heat. When the foam subsides, add the bacon. Reduce the heat to low. Add the carrots to the pan and cook the bacon and carrots together for 5 to 8 minutes, turning both the carrots and the bacon constantly with a slotted spoon. Stir in the cream, nutmeg, salt and pepper. Continue cooking for a further 3 minutes. Remove the pan from the heat.

Preheat the grill [broiler] to hot.

Arrange the carrot and bacon mixture in a medium-sized shallow, flameproof casserole or, if you prefer, in small individual ramekins. Sprinkle the cheese over the top of the mixture and place the casserole or ramekins under the grill [broiler] for 2 to 3 minutes or until the cheese melts and turns a very light golden colour. Remove from the heat, garnish with the parsley sprigs and serve.

Brussels Sprouts Polonaise

Brussels sprouts served in this way are a tasty accompaniment to roast lamb or beef or grilled [broiled] steaks.

4 SERVINGS

1½ lb. Brussels sprouts
1¼ teaspoons salt
2 hard-boiled eggs, finely chopped
2 tablespoons chopped fresh
   parsley
¼ teaspoon freshly ground black
   pepper
1½ oz. [3 tablespoons] butter
2 oz. [1 cup] fresh white breadcrumbs

With a sharp knife, trim any old or dis-

Braised Carrots and Bacon are absolutely superb.

coloured leaves from the sprouts and wash them thoroughly. Cut a cross in the base of each sprout.

Half-fill a medium-sized saucepan with water and add 1 teaspoon of the salt. Bring the water to a boil over moderately high heat. Add the sprouts. Bring the water back to the boil and cook the sprouts uncovered for 5 minutes. Cover the pan and cook the sprouts for 10 minutes longer or until they are tender but still crisp.

Drain the sprouts and transfer them to a heated serving dish. Sprinkle them with the eggs, parsley, pepper and remaining salt. Set the dish aside.

In a small saucepan, melt the butter over moderate heat. Add the breadcrumbs. Cook the mixture for 10 minutes, or until the breadcrumbs are golden, stirring occasionally with a wooden spoon.

Sprinkle the browned breadcrumbs over the sprouts and serve at once.

Mushroom Purée

A spectacularly tasty accompaniment to roast poultry, Mushroom Purée is well worth the effort required to make it.

6 SERVINGS

2½ oz. [¼ cup plus 1 tablespoon] butter
2 lb. mushrooms, wiped clean and
   sliced
3 fl. oz. [⅜ cup] water

2 teaspoons salt
2 tablespoons lemon juice
1 teaspoon grated nutmeg
½ teaspoon black pepper
2 tablespoons flour
3 fl. oz. [⅜ cup] milk
1 tablespoon chopped fresh parsley
4 to 6 croûtons

In a medium-sized frying-pan, melt 1½ ounces [3 tablespoons] of the butter over moderate heat. When the foam subsides, add the mushrooms and mix well. Pour in the water and add 1 teaspoon of the salt, the lemon juice, nutmeg and black pepper. Bring the mixture to the boil, stirring frequently. Simmer, stirring occasionally, for 8 minutes.

Remove the pan from the heat and strain the mushrooms and cooking liquid into a large mixing bowl. Reserve the cooking liquid and set aside.

Purée the mushrooms in a blender or food mill, or, alternatively, mash them with a fork. Set aside.

Add the remaining butter to the frying-pan and melt it over moderate heat. Remove the pan from the heat and, with a wooden spoon, stir in the flour to make a smooth paste. Gradually add the reserved cooking liquid and the milk, stirring constantly. Return the pan to the heat. Simmer the mixture, stirring constantly, for 2 minutes or until it is thick.

Succulent Brussels Sprouts Polonaise is a festive mixture of sprouts, eggs, parsley and breadcrumbs, cooked to perfection.

Stir the puréed mushrooms into the sauce and cook, stirring, for 2 minutes. Add the remaining salt if required.

Remove the pan from the heat and transfer the purée to a warmed serving dish. Sprinkle over the parsley and arrange the croûtons decoratively around the purée. Serve at once.

Ratatouille

☆ ① ① ✕

A classic French vegetable casserole, Ratatouille is a beautifully simple, yet delicious dish to prepare and serve. It can be eaten with steamed rice as a complete meal, as a first course, or as a vegetable accompaniment to meat or fish.

4-6 SERVINGS

1 oz. [2 tablespoons] butter
2 fl. oz. [¼ cup] olive oil
2 large onions, thinly sliced
2 garlic cloves, crushed
3 medium-sized aubergines
  [eggplants], thinly sliced and
  dégorged
1 large green pepper, white pith

removed, seeded and chopped
1 large red pepper, white pith
  removed, seeded and chopped
5 medium-sized courgettes
  [zucchini], trimmed and sliced
14 oz. canned peeled tomatoes
1 teaspoon dried basil
1 teaspoon dried rosemary
1½ teaspoons salt
¾ teaspoon freshly ground black
  pepper
2 tablespoons chopped fresh
  parsley

In a large flameproof casserole, melt the butter with the oil over moderate heat. When the foam subsides, add the onions and garlic and fry, stirring occasionally, for 5 to 7 minutes or until the onions are soft and translucent but not brown.

Add the aubergine [eggplant] slices, green and red peppers and courgette [zucchini] slices to the casserole. Fry for 5 minutes, shaking the casserole frequently. Add the tomatoes with the can juice, the basil, rosemary, salt and pepper. Sprinkle over the parsley.

Increase the heat to high and bring to the boil. Reduce the heat to low, cover the casserole and simmer for 40 to 45 minutes or until the vegetables are tender but still quite firm.

Remove the casserole from the heat and serve at once, straight from the casserole.

Salad Dressings

Coleslaw Dressing

Yogurt enlivens the flavour of this creamy salad dressing, which is particularly good with coleslaw, but can accompany any green salad.

12 FLUID OUNCES [1½ CUPS]

10 fl. oz. [1¼ cups] mayonnaise
4 tablespoons yogurt
1 teapoon sugar
½ teaspoon salt
1 tablespoon finely grated onion or spring onion [scallion]
1 tablespoon finely chopped celery

Blend the mayonnaise with the yogurt, mixing well with a wooden spoon. Add the remaining dressing ingredients and beat for 1 minute.

Use immediately.

Fines Herbes Vinaigrette

HERB DRESSING

A delicately flavoured herb dressing, Fines Herbes Vinaigrette can be made well in advance and will keep for up to a month if stored in a cool place or in the refrigerator. Serve the dressing with a tossed green salad or a tomato salad.

8 FLUID OUNCES [1 CUP]

½ teaspoon finely chopped fresh chervil
1 teaspoon finely chopped fresh chives
1 tablespoon finely chopped fresh parsley
1 teaspoon prepared French mustard
½ teaspoon salt
¼ teaspoon freshly ground black pepper
1 garlic clove, crushed
12 tablespoons olive oil
4 tablespoons tarragon vinegar
2 teaspoons lemon juice

In a small mixing bowl, combine the chervil, chives, parsley, mustard, salt, pepper and garlic with a small wooden spoon. Gradually stir in 3 tablespoons of the olive oil. Pour the contents of the bowl into a clean screw-top jar. Pour in the remaining oil, the tarragon vinegar and lemon juice.

Firmly screw on the lid. Shake the jar vigorously for 1 minute.

Unscrew the lid and pour as much of the vinaigrette as you require over your ingredients.

Replace the lid and store the remainder in a cool place or in the refrigerator until needed.

French Dressing

The classic French dressing consists of olive oil, wine vinegar, salt and pepper. Crushed garlic, mustard and/or chopped herbs may also be added, in which case the dressing becomes sauce vinaigrette, or vinaigrette dressing. The dressing may be beaten with a fork as suggested or, more conveniently, all the ingredients may be placed in a screw-top jar and then shaken thoroughly. The advantage of this method is that any extra dressing may be kept in the jar indefinitely in a cool place.

Home-made Mayonnaise—it will cheer up the dullest salad or the stodgiest sandwich.

ABOUT 4 FLUID OUNCES [½ CUP]

6 tablespoons olive oil
1 teaspoon salt
1 teaspoon freshly ground black pepper
2 tablespoons wine vinegar

In a small mixing bowl, beat the oil, salt and pepper together with a fork. Gradually beat in the vinegar. Use as required.

Honey and Vinegar Dressing

This delightfully sweet-sour dressing is excellent for serving with a plain green salad or with a chicory [French or Belgian endive] and apple salad. Any good quality wine or cider vinegar may be used.

ABOUT 6 FLUID OUNCES [¾ CUP]

1 tablespoon clear honey
5 fl. oz. [⅝ cup] vinegar
½ teaspoon salt
¼ teaspoon freshly ground black pepper
1 teaspoon finely chopped fresh chives

Place all the ingredients in a screw-top jar and shake well. Use the dressing as required.

Mayonnaise

Mayonnaise is a cold sauce made from egg yolks and oil which are beaten together to form an emulsion. The sauce is used to coat and combine cold vegetables, fish and eggs, and as a dressing with all types of salads. Once the making of the sauce is mastered, a great variety of flavourings and colourings may be added to increase its versatility (see Mayonnaise Aurore below).

If the oil is added to the egg yolks too quickly initially, and the mixture curdles, reconstitute the mixture by placing another egg yolk and the given seasonings in another bowl and beating well. Gradually add the curdled mixture to the fresh egg yolk, beating constantly until the mixture thickens, then add the mixture a little more quickly until it is all absorbed.

When making mayonnaise it is important to use fresh, unrefrigerated eggs as they have a greater ability to hold the oil in a stable emulsion.

If you wish a lighter, less rich mayonnaise, use whole eggs instead of just egg yolks.

10 FLUID OUNCES [1¼ CUPS]

2 egg yolks, at room temperature
½ teaspoon salt
¾ teaspoon dry mustard
⅛ teaspoon freshly ground white pepper
10 fl. oz. [1¼ cups] olive oil, at room temperature
1 tablespoon white wine vinegar or lemon juice

Place the egg yolks, salt, mustard and pepper in a medium-sized mixing bowl. Using a wire whisk, beat the ingredients until they are thoroughly blended and have thickened. Add the oil, a few drops at a time, whisking constantly. Do not add the oil too quickly or the mayonnaise will curdle.

After the mayonnaise has thickened the oil may be added a little more rapidly.

Beat in a few drops of vinegar or lemon juice from time to time to prevent the mayonnaise from becoming too thick. When all of the oil has been added, stir in the remaining wine vinegar or lemon juice.

Taste the sauce for seasoning and add more salt, mustard and wine vinegar if desired.

MAYONNAISE AURORE
Add 2 tablespoons of tomato purée, 1 tablespoon of single [light] cream and 2 drops of Worcestershire sauce to the mayonnaise.

Mint Dressing

A cool, refreshing, slightly tart dressing, Mint Dressing is perfect spooned over cold cooked lamb, roast beef or on a tomato or potato salad.

ABOUT 2 FLUID OUNCES [¼ CUP]

3 tablespoons olive oil
1 tablespoon lemon juice
½ teaspoon salt
½ teaspoon freshly ground black pepper
1 tablespoon finely chopped fresh mint
2 teaspoons sugar

In a small mixing bowl, combine the olive oil, lemon juice, salt, black pepper, mint and sugar and mix well with a wooden spoon. Alternatively place all the ingredients in a screw-top jar and shake well to blend.

Place the dressing in the refrigerator to chill for at least 30 minutes before serving.

Roquefort Dressing

Serve this deliciously different salad dressing with a mixed green salad, or with a cold fish dish.

ABOUT 8 FLUID OUNCES [1 CUP]

6 fl. oz. [¾ cup] olive oil
2 teaspoons salt
2 teaspoons freshly ground black pepper
2 fl. oz. [¼ cup] wine vinegar
2 oz. Roquefort cheese, finely crumbled
1 tablespoon chopped fresh chives

In a medium-sized mixing bowl, beat the oil, salt and pepper together with a fork. Gradually beat in the vinegar, then mash in the cheese until the mixture is thoroughly combined. Stir in the chives.

Either use the dressing immediately or pour it into a screw-top jar and chill in the refrigerator until required.

Thousand Island Dressing

A salad dressing with a mayonnaise base, Thousand Island Dressing is thought to have originated in the United States. It is particularly excellent served with mixed vegetable salads, and of course, with hamburgers.

ABOUT 1 PINT [2½ CUPS]

16 fl. oz. [2 cups] mayonnaise
1¼ teaspoons Tabasco sauce
2 tablespoons chopped pimientos or sweet pickle
10 stuffed green olives, finely chopped
2 hard-boiled eggs, very finely chopped
1 medium-sized shallot, very finely chopped
3 tablespoons olive oil
½ teaspoon salt
½ teaspoon freshly ground black pepper
1 tablespoon wine vinegar

In a large bowl, combine the mayonnaise, Tabasco, chopped pimientos or pickle, green olives, chopped eggs, shallot, olive oil, salt, black pepper and wine vinegar and beat them together with a wooden spoon, until they are thoroughly blended.

Pour the dressing into a serving bowl and chill in the refrigerator for at least 1 hour before serving.

Yogurt Dressing

Serve Yogurt Dressing with salads as an interesting alternative to mayonnaise or vinaigrette, or as an accompaniment to fried vegetables or kebabs.

ABOUT 12 FLUID OUNCES [1½ CUPS]

12 fl. oz. [1½ cups] yogurt
juice of 1 lemon
1 garlic clove, crushed
1 teaspoon salt
1 teaspoon black pepper

Place all the ingredients in a medium-sized mixing bowl and beat them together with a fork until they are thoroughly combined.

The dressing is now ready to use.

Cabbage, Pepper and Onion Salad

This tasty and attractive Cabbage, Pepper and Onion Salad is ideal to serve with meat or chicken when salad greens are not available.

8 SERVINGS

1 large red pepper, white pith removed, seeded and finely sliced
1 large green pepper, white pith removed, seeded and finely sliced
6 to 8 spring onions [scallions], finely chopped
1 cucumber, cut into ½-inch cubes
1 lb. tomatoes, finely sliced
½ white cabbage, coarse outer leaves removed, washed and finely sliced
2 tablespoons clear honey
juice of 1 lemon
10 tablespoons olive or vegetable oil
4 tablespoons vinegar
2 teaspoons salt
1 teaspoon freshly ground black pepper

Combine the peppers, spring onions [scallions], cucumber, tomatoes and cabbage in a large salad bowl.

Put the honey, lemon juice, oil, vinegar, salt and pepper into a screw-top jar and shake it until the dressing is well mixed.

Pour the dressing over the salad just before serving and toss well.

Chef's Salad

An excellent way to use leftover meats and vegetables, Chef's Salad makes an appetizing supper or luncheon entrée. Turkey and ham may be substituted for the meats suggested in the recipe below, and vegetables such as asparagus tips, cold cooked peas, cooked French beans or beetroot [beet] may be used rather than cheese and egg as in this recipe.

4 SERVINGS

1 medium-sized lettuce, outer leaves removed, washed and chilled
3 oz. cold, cooked chicken, cut in strips about 4 inches by ½ inch
3 oz. cold, cooked tongue, cut in strips about 4 inches by ½ inch
3 oz. Gruyère cheese, cut into pieces
1 hard-boiled egg, very thinly sliced
1 tablespoon finely chopped onion
3 tablespoons stoned, chopped black olives
6 tablespoons olive oil
2 tablespoons red wine vinegar
½ teaspoon lemon juice
¼ teaspoon prepared French mustard
1 teaspoon salt
½ teaspoon freshly ground black pepper

Place the lettuce leaves in a large salad bowl. Add the chicken, tongue, cheese, egg, onion and olives.

In a screw-top jar, combine the olive oil, vinegar, lemon juice, mustard, salt and pepper, and shake the jar vigorously until all of the ingredients are well blended.

Pour the dressing over the salad, and place the bowl in the refrigerator to chill for 10 minutes. Just before serving, toss the salad well.

Cucumber and Grape Salad

Cucumber and grapes set in a tangy lemon-flavoured jelly [gelatin] is a refreshing salad

Cabbage, Pepper and Onion Salad is economical and super to eat.

and makes an attractive addition to a summer buffet.

6 SERVINGS

1 large cucumber, peeled and thinly sliced
1 lb. green grapes, washed, halved and seeded
15 fl. oz. [1⅞ cups] water
5 oz. packet lemon jelly [gelatin]
3 tablespoons orange juice
5 tablespoons lemon juice
1 tablespoon very finely chopped onion
⅛ teaspoon cayenne pepper
½ teaspoon salt
¼ teaspoon freshly ground black pepper
1 Webb [iceberg] lettuce, outer leaves removed, washed and shredded

MARINADE

3 tablespoons olive oil
1 tablespoon wine vinegar
¼ teaspoon salt
¼ teaspoon freshly ground black pepper
¼ teaspoon dry mustard

To prepare the marinade, in a medium-sized bowl, combine the oil, vinegar, salt, pepper and mustard, beating with a fork until all the ingredients are blended.

Place the cucumber slices and grapes in the bowl and marinate them for at least 30 minutes or until you are ready to use them.

In a small saucepan, bring 5 fluid ounces [⅝ cup] of the water to the boil over moderate heat. Remove the pan from the heat and add the jelly [gelatin]. Stir until the jelly [gelatin] has dissolved. Stir in the remaining water. Stir in the orange and lemon juice, onion, cayenne, salt and pepper. Cool the jelly [gelatin] until it is almost set. With a slotted spoon, remove the grapes and cucumber slices from the

Cucumber and Grape Salad makes a refreshing buffet centrepiece.

marinade. Drain them thoroughly on kitchen paper towels and then add most of them to the jelly [gelatin]. Reserve the marinade and the remaining grapes and cucumber slices for the garnish.

Spoon the jelly [gelatin] into a 2½-pint [1½-quart] mould. Cover the mould with plastic wrap or aluminium foil and put it in the refrigerator to chill for 3 to 4 hours or until the jelly [gelatin] is completely set.

Arrange the lettuce on a serving dish. Quickly dip the mould into hot water and turn the jelly [gelatin] out on to the lettuce. Arrange the reserved grapes and cucumber slices around the salad and pour a little of the reserved marinade over them.

Serve at once.

Fennel, Watercress, Cucumber and Tomato Salad

Delicious Fennel, Watercress, Cucumber and Tomato Salad is a meal in itself — try it for lunch with lots of crusty bread and a glass of milk.

4 SERVINGS

1 bunch watercress, washed and shaken dry
½ fennel, trimmed and sliced
½ small cucumber, thinly sliced
4 tomatoes, quartered
6 anchovy fillets, halved
1 spring onion [scallion], trimmed and finely chopped
2 tablespoons finely chopped pimiento
3 fl. oz. [⅜ cup] French dressing

In a large, deep serving platter or salad bowl, combine all the ingredients except the French dressing, tossing with two spoons until they are well mixed.

Pour the French dressing into the mixture and, using the spoons, gently toss until all the ingredients are well coated. Serve at once.

Fruit and Vegetable Salad

This beautiful salad is ideal to serve at a summer buffet. Alternatively, it may be eaten as a light meal on its own.

4-6 SERVINGS

4 oz. canned pineapple chunks, drained
8 oz. small seedless green grapes
2 fresh peaches, peeled, stoned and sliced
2 carrots, scraped and grated
1 small green pepper, white pith removed, seeded and thinly sliced
2 spring onions [scallions], finely chopped
6 radishes, sliced
5 fl. oz. [⅝ cup] French dressing, made with lemon juice instead of

Delicious Fennel, Watercress, Cucumber and Tomato Salad tastes even better than it looks!

vinegar
1 cos [romaine] lettuce, outer leaves removed, washed and shredded

In a medium-sized mixing bowl, carefully combine the pineapple, grapes, peaches, carrots, green pepper, spring onions [scallions], radishes and French dressing.

Arrange the shredded lettuce leaves around the outer edge of a shallow serving dish and pile the fruit and vegetable mixture in the centre. Serve immediately.

Greek Salad

A simple dish using Greek feta cheese, this salad is very colourful and can be served on its own for lunch or as an accompaniment to a cold savoury flan or pie. The dressing

24

should not be added to the salad until just before serving.

4-6 SERVINGS

1 cos [romaine] lettuce, outer leaves removed, washed and separated into leaves
1 bunch radishes, cleaned and sliced
8 oz. feta cheese, cut into cubes
¼ teaspoon dried marjoram
4 tomatoes, blanched, peeled and sliced
6 anchovies, drained and finely chopped
6 large black olives, halved and stoned
1 tablespoon chopped fresh parsley
½ teaspoon freshly ground black pepper
DRESSING
4 tablespoons olive oil
1½ tablespoons white wine vinegar
1 tablespoon chopped mixed fresh herbs, such as marjoram, chives or lemon thyme
4 spring onions [scallions], chopped
1 teaspoon sugar
¼ teaspoon salt
½ teaspoon freshly ground black pepper

Tear the lettuce leaves into pieces and arrange them on a large dish. Scatter the radish slices over the lettuce. Arrange the cheese in the centre of the dish and sprinkle it with the marjoram. Place the tomatoes in a circle around the cheese and put the anchovies on top of the tomatoes, alternating with the olives. Sprinkle the parsley and pepper on top.

In a small bowl, mix together the oil, vinegar, fresh herbs, spring onions [scallions], sugar, salt and pepper.

Pour the dressing over the salad and serve.

Gruyère and Mushroom Salad

Light and refreshing, Gruyère and Mushroom Salad perfectly complements roasts and grilled [broiled] meats, especially the lighter meats such as veal and lamb.

4 SERVINGS

8 oz. Gruyère cheese, cut into small cubes
4 oz. button mushrooms, wiped clean and quartered
4 large lettuce leaves, washed and shaken dry
1 tablespoon chopped fresh parsley
DRESSING
6 tablespoons olive oil
2 tablespoons red wine vinegar

1 garlic clove, crushed
½ teaspoon salt
¼ teaspoon freshly ground black pepper

First, make the dressing. In a medium-sized mixing bowl, combine all the dressing ingredients, beating with a fork until they are well blended. Set aside.

In a medium-sized bowl, combine the cheese and mushrooms. Pour over the dressing and, using two large spoons, toss the cheese and mushrooms until they are well coated. Set aside to marinate for 20 minutes.

Line the bottom of a shallow salad bowl or four individual serving plates with the lettuce leaves. Spoon the cheese and mushroom mixture on top and sprinkle over the parsley. Serve immediately.

Korean Vegetable Salad

This attractive crunchy salad may be served as a delicious accompaniment to roast pork or as an unusual first course.

4 SERVINGS

1 small turnip, peeled
1 teaspoon salt
2 to 4 tablespoons vegetable oil
1 small onion, finely chopped
4 oz. mushrooms, wiped clean and thinly sliced
2 celery stalks, thinly sliced

Tasty Gruyère and Mushroom Salad.

3 spring onions [scallions], chopped
1 carrot, scraped and sliced
1 tablespoon chopped pine nuts
DRESSING
3 tablespoons soy sauce
1 tablespoon soft brown sugar
1 tablespoon vinegar
¼ teaspoon black pepper
¼ teaspoon ground ginger

With a sharp knife, cut the turnip into long, thin strips. Sprinkle the strips with the salt and set aside for 15 minutes.

In a small frying-pan, heat 2 tablespoons of the oil over moderate heat. When the oil is hot, add the turnip strips. Fry for 3 to 4 minutes, turning occasionally or until they are crisp. Transfer the strips to kitchen paper towels to drain.

Add the onion to the pan and fry, stirring occasionally, for 8 to 10 minutes, or until it is golden brown. Transfer the onion to kitchen paper towels to drain.

Add the mushrooms to the pan, with more oil if necessary, and fry, stirring frequently, for 4 minutes. Transfer the mushrooms to kitchen paper towels to drain.

Fry the celery for 2 to 3 minutes, or until it is gold. Transfer the celery to kitchen paper towels to drain.

When the fried vegetables are cold, combine them with the spring onions [scallions] and carrot in a serving dish. Sprinkle the pine nuts on top.

In a screw-top jar, combine the soy sauce, sugar, vinegar, pepper and ginger. Shake well and pour the dressing over the vegetables. Serve at once.

25

Melon and Avocado Salad

Melon and Avocado Salad is an unusual combination for a savoury salad. It is the perfect accompaniment to grilled [broiled] lamb chops or steak. This dish can also be served as a first course.

4 SERVINGS

2 medium-sized avocados, halved and stoned
1 tablespoon lemon juice
½ medium-sized honeydew melon, seeded
½ teaspoon finely chopped fresh tarragon or ¼ teaspoon dried tarragon
DRESSING
6 tablespoons olive oil
½ teaspoon salt
¼ teaspoon black pepper
2 tablespoons lemon juice

With a small melon baller, scoop out the avocado flesh to within ⅛-inch of the skin. Reserve the avocado shells. Place the avocado balls in a medium-sized mixing bowl and sprinkle over the tablespoon of lemon juice. Set aside.

Scoop out the melon flesh in the same way and add the melon balls to the avocado balls. Place the bowl in the refrigerator to chill while you make the dressing.

In a small mixing bowl, beat the oil, salt and pepper together with a fork. Gradually add the lemon juice.

Remove the melon and avocado from the refrigerator and pour over the dressing. With a wooden spoon carefully toss the ingredients together until the balls are well coated. Serve at once.

Mushroom and Bacon Salad

Mushroom and Bacon Salad may be served as part of an hors d'oeuvre, as an accompaniment to grilled [broiled] meat or as part of a large mixed salad.

4 SERVINGS

8 oz. button mushrooms, wiped clean and thinly sliced
4 streaky bacon slices, rinds removed
1 celery stalk, trimmed and finely chopped
1 tablespoon chopped fresh parsley
1 tablespoon chopped fresh chives
DRESSING
6 tablespoons olive oil
2 tablespoons white wine vinegar
½ teaspoon salt
¼ teaspoon freshly ground black pepper

First make the dressing. In a medium-sized mixing bowl, combine all the dressing ingredients, beating with a fork until they are well blended. Add the sliced mushrooms and set aside to marinate for 30 minutes.

Meanwhile, preheat the grill [broiler] to high.

Place the bacon slices on a rack in the grill [broiler] pan and grill [broil] the bacon, turning once, for 5 minutes, or until it is crisp. Remove the bacon from the grill [broiler] and set aside to drain and cool on kitchen paper towels.

Crumble the bacon into the mushroom mixture and add the celery, parsley and

Unusual Mussel, Hake and Vegetable Salad is served hot.

chives. Mix well. Transfer to a serving dish and serve immediately.

Mussel, Hake and Vegetable Salad

A delightful hot salad Mussel, Hake and Vegetable Salad may be served with crusty bread and butter for an hors d'oeuvre or light meal.

4-6 SERVINGS

4 fl. oz. [½ cup] olive oil
¼ teaspoon hot chilli powder
2 tablespoons chopped fresh parsley
¼ teaspoon dried thyme
1 bay leaf
2 garlic cloves, crushed
1½ lb. hake, cut into 6 x 1-inch slices
4 oz. frozen petits pois, thawed, cooked until tender and drained
3 canned red pimientos, drained and cut into strips
24 mussels, scrubbed and steamed
GARNISH
8 croûtons, kept hot
2 hard-boiled eggs, quartered

In a shallow ovenproof dish large enough to hold the fish slices in one layer, combine the olive oil, chilli powder, parsley, thyme, bay leaf and garlic. Place the fish in the dish and marinate at room temperature for 1 hour, basting occasionally.

Preheat the oven to fairly hot 375°F (Gas Mark 5, 190°C).

Cover the dish tightly and place it in the oven. Bake for 15 minutes.

Remove the dish from the oven. Uncover and place the petits pois, pimientos and mussels in the dish. Return it to the oven and bake for a further 5 to 10 minutes or until the fish flakes easily when tested with a fork.

Remove the dish from the oven. Remove and discard the bay leaf.

Garnish with the croûtons and hardboiled eggs and serve immediately.

Nun's Salad

A simple dish, Nun's Salad is so called because of the use of black and white ingredients. Serve it as a light supper dish or as a first course.

4 SERVINGS

1 lb. cooked chicken, diced
12 spring onions [scallions], white part only, chopped
1 lb. potatoes, peeled, cooked and diced
2 oz. [⅓ cup] seedless raisins
8 oz. large black grapes, halved and seeded
2 oz. [⅔ cup] large black olives, halved and stoned
½ teaspoon salt
¼ teaspoon freshly ground black pepper
1 large apple, peeled, cored and diced
6 fl. oz. [¾ cup] mayonnaise

In a large salad bowl, combine the chicken, spring onions [scallions], potatoes, raisins, half the grapes, the olives, salt, pepper and apple. Pour over the mayonnaise and, using two large spoons, toss the salad, mixing the ingredients together thoroughly.

Arrange the remaining grape halves decoratively over the top. Place the bowl in the refrigerator and chill the salad for 30 minutes before serving.

Good to look at, satisfying to eat, Nun's Salad makes an excellent summer supper for the family.

Potato Salad

This simple Potato Salad with mayonnaise dressing may be served with cold meat or as one of a selection of salads. Use the green part of the leeks for this recipe and save the white parts for future use.

4 SERVINGS

1 lb. potatoes, cooked, peeled and sliced
4 fl. oz. [½ cup] mayonnaise
1 tablespoon lemon juice
1 tablespoon olive oil
½ teaspoon salt
½ teaspoon freshly ground black pepper
2 tablespoons finely chopped fresh chives
4 tablespoons finely chopped leeks

Place three-quarters of the potatoes in a medium-sized mixing bowl. Pour over the mayonnaise and sprinkle with the lemon juice, oil, salt, pepper and 1 tablespoon of chives. Using two large spoons, carefully toss the potatoes until they are thoroughly coated with the mayonnaise mixture.

Spoon the mixture into a serving bowl. Arrange the remaining potato slices over the top of the salad. Sprinkle with the remaining chives and scatter the leeks around the edge of the bowl.

Cover the bowl and place it in the refrigerator to chill for 30 minutes before serving.

Potato, Beef and Tomato Salad

Potato, Beef and Tomato Salad is a delicious salad with a sour cream and horse-radish sauce. Serve with crusty bread and a chilled Tavel Rosé wine for a perfect spring supper or lunch.

4 SERVINGS

1 small lettuce, outer leaves removed, washed and separated into leaves
2 lb. cold roast beef, cubed
4 medium-sized cold cooked potatoes, cubed
4 medium-sized tomatoes, blanched, peeled, seeded and quartered
4 pickled gherkins, sliced
2 hard-boiled eggs, thinly sliced
¼ teaspoon paprika
SAUCE
12 fl. oz. [1½ cups] sour cream
3 tablespoons cold horseradish sauce
½ teaspoon salt

½ teaspoon white pepper

Arrange the lettuce leaves decoratively on a large, shallow serving plate and set aside.

In a large mixing bowl, combine the meat, potatoes, tomatoes and gherkins. Set aside.

In a small bowl, mix the sour cream, horseradish sauce, salt and pepper together, beating until they are well blended.

Spoon the sauce over the meat mixture and, using two spoons, carefully toss to coat well.

Arrange the meat mixture on the lettuce leaves. Garnish with the egg slices and sprinkle over the paprika. Serve at once.

Rice and Ham Salad

Rice and Ham Salad is a delicious ham, fruit, vegetable and rice salad which makes a refreshingly different summer lunch or dinner. Made in a smaller quantity, the salad can be used as a superb stuffing for avocados or large fresh tomatoes.

4 SERVINGS

8 oz. [1⅓ cups] long-grain rice, washed, soaked in cold water for 30 minutes and drained
1 teaspoon salt
4 very thick slices cooked, lean ham, diced
4 canned pineapple rings, drained and chopped
2 medium-sized green peppers, white pith removed, seeded and coarsely chopped
1 red eating apple, cored and chopped
DRESSING
1 egg yolk, at room temperature
¼ teaspoon salt
½ teaspoon dry mustard
⅛ teaspoon white pepper
4 fl. oz. [½ cup] olive oil, at room temperature
1 tablespoon lemon juice
2 fl. oz. double cream [¼ cup heavy cream]
¼ teaspoon cayenne pepper
1 tablespoon finely chopped fresh chives

Place the rice, salt and enough water just to cover the rice in a medium-sized saucepan. Set the pan over high heat and bring the water to the boil. Reduce the heat to very low, cover the pan and simmer for 15 minutes, or until all the water has been absorbed and the rice is tender.

Remove the pan from the heat and set the rice aside to cool completely.

To make the dressing, place the egg yolk, salt, mustard and pepper in a

medium-sized mixing bowl. Using a wire whisk, beat the ingredients until they are thoroughly blended. Add the oil, a few drops at a time, whisking constantly. Do not add the oil too quickly or the mayonnaise will curdle. After the mayonnaise has thickened the oil may be added a little more rapidly. Beat in a few drops of the lemon juice from time to time to prevent the mayonnaise from becoming too thick. When all the oil has been added, stir in the remaining lemon juice. Taste for seasoning and add more salt, mustard or lemon juice if desired.

Stir in the cream, cayenne and chives and blend well.

Add the ham, pineapple, green peppers, apple and the rice to the dressing. Toss the ingredients thoroughly. Turn the salad out into a medium-sized serving bowl. Place it in the refrigerator to chill for 30 minutes before serving.

Tomato and French Bean Salad

The combination of red and green in Tomato and French Bean Salad makes it colourful as well as delicious. This salad is very good with cold meats and has the advantage that it may be prepared well in advance of serving.

6-8 SERVINGS

1 lb. tomatoes, very thinly sliced and seeded
1 lb. French beans, trimmed, cooked and drained
DRESSING
3 tablespoons wine vinegar
6 tablespoons olive oil
¼ teaspoon salt
¼ teaspoon freshly ground black pepper
½ teaspoon prepared French mustard
½ teaspoon sugar
1 garlic clove, crushed

Place all the dressing ingredients in a screw-top jar and shake vigorously until they are well mixed. Set the dressing aside.

Place the tomatoes and beans in a large serving dish and pour over the dressing. Using two large spoons, toss the salad until the vegetables are thoroughly coated with the dressing.

Chill the salad in the refrigerator before serving.

Easy to make, even easier to eat, Potato Salad is a favourite dish throughout the world.

Salads for Special Occasions

Caesar Salad

 ①

This unusual salad comes from the United States where it is eaten on its own as a light lunch dish, or served with grilled [broiled] steak, or fish.

4 SERVINGS

- 5 fl. oz. [⅝ cup] olive oil
- 4 thick slices white bread, crusts removed and cut into cubes
- 1 garlic clove
- 1½ teaspoons salt
- 2 tablespoons wine vinegar
- 1 teaspoon lemon juice
- ½ teaspoon Worcestershire sauce
- ¼ teaspoon prepared mustard
- ⅛ teaspoon sugar
- ¼ teaspoon black pepper
- 2 heads cos [romaine] lettuce, washed and dried
- 6 anchovy fillets, cut in small pieces
- 1 egg, cooked in boiling water for 1 minute
- 2 oz. [½ cup] Parmesan cheese, grated

Heat 2 fluid ounces [¼ cup] of the olive oil in a large, heavy frying-pan over moderately high heat. Fry the bread cubes in the oil for 10 to 15 minutes or until crisp, turning frequently with a spoon. Remove the croûtons from the pan and drain them on kitchen paper towels.

Mash the garlic together with the salt in the bottom of a large salad bowl. Add the remaining olive oil, the vinegar, lemon juice, Worcestershire sauce, mustard, sugar and the pepper and mix well.

Tear the lettuce into bite-sized pieces and add to the salad bowl with the anchovies. Toss well with the dressing.

Break the egg over the top of the salad, add the croûtons and Parmesan cheese and toss the salad again. Serve immediately.

Russian Salad

 ①

Russian Salad (pictured on page 1) is a selection of cooked vegetables and meat coated in mayonnaise. Served with meat as suggested here, Russian Salad makes an excellent main course with crusty bread and a well-chilled white wine. Alternatively, the meat is often omitted and the salad served as a substantial side dish.

4-8 SERVINGS

- 3 large cooked potatoes, diced
- 4 medium-sized cooked carrots, diced
- 4 oz. cooked French beans, halved
- 1 small onion, very finely chopped

- 4 oz. cooked fresh peas, weighed after shelling
- 2 oz. cooked tongue, diced
- 4 oz. cooked chicken, diced
- 2 oz. garlic sausage, diced
- 8 fl. oz. [1 cup] mayonnaise
- ¼ teaspoon cayenne pepper

GARNISH
- 2 hard-boiled eggs, sliced
- 1 cooked beetroot [beet], sliced
- 2 gherkins, thinly sliced

In a large salad bowl, combine all of the salad ingredients except the mayonnaise and cayenne. Set aside.

In a small bowl, beat the mayonnaise and cayenne together with a fork until they are well blended. Spoon the mayonnaise into the salad bowl and toss well.

Garnish the salad with the eggs, beetroot [beet] and gherkins and chill in the refrigerator for 15 to 20 minutes before serving.

Salade Niçoise
POTATO, FRENCH BEAN AND TOMATO SALAD

 ① ①

Salade Niçoise is one of the great classic dishes of regional France and its succulent

mixture of potatoes, French beans, tomatoes, anchovies and capers in a spicy French dressing evokes the warmth of its city of origin. Tuna fish is often added to the salad, both in France and outside, although strictly speaking this is not traditional. With the addition of tuna fish, however, and accompanied by crusty bread and lots of well-chilled Provençal white wine, it makes a delightful meal.

3-6 SERVINGS

- 1 small lettuce, outer leaves removed, washed and separated into leaves
- 6 medium-sized cold cooked potatoes, diced
- 10 oz. cold cooked French beans, cut into ½-inch lengths
- 6 tomatoes, blanched, peeled and quartered
- 4 fl. oz. [½ cup] French dressing

GARNISH
- 6 anchovy fillets, halved
- 10 black olives, stoned
- 2 tablespoons capers

A classic Salad from France, Salade Niçoise is a blend of potatoes, French beans and tomatoes, garnished with anchovies and olives.

Arrange the lettuce leaves decoratively on a large, shallow serving plate and set aside.

In a large mixing bowl, combine the potatoes, beans and tomatoes. Pour over the French dressing and, using two spoons, carefully toss the vegetables until they are thoroughly coated.

Spoon the vegetables on to the lettuce leaves and garnish with the anchovy fillets, olives and capers. Serve at once.

Salmagundy

Salmagundy is a traditional British salad, popular in the seventeenth and eighteenth centuries, which is built up like a small pyramid, with different, brightly coloured ingredients. The salad can be garnished with parsley, tomatoes and lemon and orange segments. A very large round plate is required on which to serve the salad, and a shallow pudding basin or large saucer is inverted and placed on the plate, to give a base upon which to build the salad. The butter 'statue' is traditional to the dish, but it may be omitted, if preferred.

8-10 SERVINGS

1 teaspoon vegetable oil
½ medium-sized curly endive [chicory], coarse outer leaves removed, washed, shaken dry and shredded
1 lb. cooked chicken meat, sliced
1 lb. lean cooked tongue, sliced
6 hard-boiled eggs, separated and finely chopped
8 rollmops or pickled herrings, drained
2 large tomatoes, quartered
1 large lemon, quartered
1 large orange, quartered
1 small cooked beetroot [beet], finely chopped
8 black olives, stoned
1 small dill pickle, finely chopped
8 tablespoons chopped fresh watercress
8 oz. [1 cup] butter, frozen in 1 piece

With the oil, lightly grease the outside of a shallow pudding basin or large saucer and place it, inverted, on a large round serving plate.

Sprinkle the endive [chicory] over the saucer.

Salmagundy makes an extra special treat for the family.

Arrange the chicken slices around the edge of the serving plate and then, inside, make another slightly smaller circle with the tongue. Make a circle with the chopped egg yolks. Arrange the herrings inside the egg yolk circle and place a tomato quarter between each herring. Make a circle with the egg whites. Make a circle with the lemon and orange quarters, arranging them alternately.

Sprinkle the beetroot [beet], olives and dill pickle around the edge of the endive [chicory] on the basin or saucer. Make a circle around the outer edge of the plate with the watercress. Place the plate in the refrigerator and chill for at least 30 minutes.

Place the butter on a wooden board. Using a small sharp knife, carve the butter into a decorative shape, such as a flower, fruit or bird.

Remove the plate from the refrigerator. Place the butter decoration in the centre of the endive [chicory].

Serve at once.

Sour Cream Chicken Salad

The secret of Sour Cream Chicken Salad is in the attractive presentation. The colourful ingredients make it look pretty as well as tasty to eat. Serve for a special family meal with lots of crusty bread and some well-chilled white wine such as Hungarian Riesling.

4-6 SERVINGS

1 x 4 lb. cooked chicken, cold
6 medium-sized hard-boiled eggs
2 green peppers, white pith removed, seeded and finely shredded
4 tablespoons stuffed green olives, sliced
1 lb. green grapes, peeled and seeded
4 oz. [1 cup] blanched sliced almonds
½ teaspoon freshly ground black pepper

FRENCH DRESSING

3 tablespoons white wine vinegar
2 teaspoons prepared French mustard
½ teaspoon salt
½ teaspoon freshly ground black pepper
6 tablespoons olive oil

SOUR CREAM DRESSING

6 tablespoons white wine vinegar
10 fl. oz. [1¼ cups] sour cream
2 teaspoons sugar
½ teaspoon salt
½ teaspoon freshly ground white pepper

On a wooden board, carve the chicken into pieces and, with a small, sharp knife, detach the meat from the skin and bones. Discard the skin and bones. Cut the meat into thin strips and put them into a salad bowl.

Separate the yolks from the whites of the hard-boiled eggs. Finely chop the whites and add to the chicken. Keep the egg yolks aside on a plate. Add the green peppers, olives, grapes and almonds. Do not mix or toss the ingredients. Set the salad bowl aside.

Prepare the French dressing. In a small mixing bowl, combine the vinegar,

Sour Cream Chicken Salad makes an especially delightful summer meal, served with crusty bread and well chilled white wine.

mustard, salt and pepper. With a large spoon, beat the ingredients together to mix well, then stir in the olive oil. Pour the dressing over the ingredients in the salad bowl.

Press the egg yolks through a fine strainer or push them through a garlic press over the chicken mixture. Toss the salad to mix the ingredients well. Sprinkle the black pepper over the top. Cover the salad bowl and keep it in the refrigerator until you are ready to serve it.

Lastly prepare the sour cream dressing. In a small mixing bowl, slowly beat the vinegar into the sour cream. Add the sugar, salt and pepper and mix well. Taste the dressing and add more salt, sugar, vinegar or white pepper, if necessary. Pour the dressing into a sauce boat or small serving bowl.

Serve the salad, accompanied by the sour cream dressing.

Vegetables and salads for entertaining

Vegetables and salads tend to be a bit neglected when you're planning a 'special' meal; with all that energy about to be expended on a fancier meat or fish dish, perhaps a dessert as well, there usually isn't much time (or inclination) for anything else. Which is a pity because a well-chosen accompaniment or two can make the difference between a merely acceptable meal and a spectacularly successful one — and just in case you need convincing of this, we recommend that you check (and preferably try) our fabulous recipes for Celery with Almonds (page 41), Légumes Nouveaux Flambés (pictured below, page 49) and Cabbage and Sesame Seed Salad (page 62).

Vegetables and salads can also make more than palatable meals on their own — and are in fact often much more suitable for informal entertaining than heavier, more conventional meals centred around meat. For light but elegant occasions, for instance, you could serve Artichokes Stuffed with Pork and Almonds (page 34); Boston Baked Beans (page 50), on the other hand, is probably the ultimate — and perfect — special dish to serve to any guest under the age of 12, and Rice Salad with Garlic Sausage (page 59) makes a perfect offering for a summer supper.

Most of the recipes which follow have been specially chosen for their ease of preparation, always a consideration since it's a dire fate indeed to be too tired to sit down and enjoy your own dinner parties. Nor will any of them break the bank, especially if the ingredients are bought (as all fresh vegetables and fruit should be for the best results) on a seasonal basis.

So — lots of luck, lots of happy experimenting and, most especially, lots of very good eating!

Artichokes Stuffed with Pork and Almonds

This is an unusual and rather expensive way to serve artichokes although it may be served as a main course rather than as a vegetable accompaniment. Serve with some melted butter, into which the artichoke leaves and hearts can be dipped.

4 SERVINGS

4 large artichokes
2 fl. oz. [¼ cup] lemon juice
   enough boiling water to cover the artichokes
1 tablespoon salt
STUFFING
2 oz. [¼ cup] vegetable fat
8 oz. minced [ground] pork
1 medium-sized onion, chopped
2 oz. [1 cup] fresh white breadcrumbs
2 tablespoons chopped fresh parsley
½ teaspoon salt
¼ teaspoon black pepper
½ teaspoon celery salt
2½ oz. [½ cup] blanched almonds, finely chopped
1 egg, lightly beaten
1 tablespoon vegetable oil

Wash and prepare the artichokes for boiling. Pour a little lemon juice over the cut areas to prevent them from discolouring. Using a sharp knife, cut off the top third of each artichoke. Pull open the centre leaves carefully and pull out the yellow and purple leaves from the centre. Using a teaspoon, scrape and pull off all the fuzzy chokes to expose the heart. Pour a little lemon into the hollows. Push the leaves back together again.

Stand the artichokes in a large saucepan. If they do not fit snugly into the saucepan, tie a piece of string around each one so they will keep their shape while boiling.

Pour the boiling water and the remaining lemon juice over the artichokes so that they are completely covered. Add the salt. Cover the saucepan and simmer the artichokes over moderately low heat for 25 minutes, or until the bases are tender when pierced with a sharp knife. When the artichokes are cooked, with a slotted spoon remove them from the water and turn them upside down in a colander to drain.

While the artichokes are boiling, preheat the oven to moderate 350°F (Gas Mark 4, 180°C). To make the stuffing, in a large, heavy frying-pan, melt the fat over moderate heat. When the foam subsides, add the pork and onion and fry, stirring occasionally, for 5 to 7 minutes

or until the onion is soft and translucent but not brown. Remove the frying-pan from the heat and add the breadcrumbs, parsley, salt, pepper, celery salt, almonds and beaten egg. Stir the mixture thoroughly with a wooden spoon.

Place the artichokes in a baking dish and fill the centres with the stuffing.

Pour a little water around the artichokes and brush them generously with the oil. Cover the dish with aluminium foil and bake in the oven for 30 to 40 minutes or until the artichokes and fillings are cooked and tender.

Serve hot.

Artichoke Hearts in Butter

This simple, well-flavoured dish may be served either as a first course or as an accompaniment to lighter meats, such as chicken, lamb or veal.

4 SERVINGS

2 tablespoons lemon juice
12 artichoke hearts
4 oz. [½ cup] butter
4 tablespoons chopped shallots or spring onions [scallions]
½ teaspoon salt
¼ teaspoon freshly ground white pepper
1½ tablespoons chopped fresh parsley

Half-fill a large saucepan with water and add the lemon juice. Place the pan over moderately high heat and bring the water to the boil. Reduce the heat to low, add the artichoke hearts and simmer them for 10 minutes or until they are tender. Remove the artichoke hearts from the pan and drain them in a colander. Cut them into quarters, then set the quarters aside.

Meanwhile, preheat the oven to warm 325°F (Gas Mark 3, 170°C).

In a medium-sized flameproof casserole, melt the butter over moderate heat. When the foam subsides, add the shallots or spring onions [scallions] and artichoke hearts, and cook, stirring, for 1 or 2 minutes or until the hearts are well coated with the butter. Sprinkle over the salt and pepper.

Cover the casserole and cook in the oven for 15 minutes. Remove the casserole from the oven, sprinkle over the parsley and serve at once.

Artichokes Stuffed with Pork and Almonds – elegant to look at, marvellous to eat – makes a festive lunch or supper dish.

Artichoke Hearts with Cream

This smooth vegetable dish is particularly delicious served with roast leg of lamb or pork.

4 SERVINGS

2 oz. [¼ cup] butter
12 artichoke hearts, cooked as in the previous recipe and cut into quarters
1 teaspoon salt
½ teaspoon white pepper
8 fl. oz. double cream [1 cup heavy cream]
1 tablespoon lemon juice
½ teaspoon grated nutmeg

In a medium-sized saucepan, melt the

butter over moderate heat. When the foam subsides, add the artichoke hearts and, with a wooden spoon, baste them thoroughly in the melted butter. Stir in half of the salt and pepper. Reduce the heat to low, cover the pan and simmer the artichoke hearts for 10 minutes or until they are thoroughly heated through.

Meanwhile, in a small, heavy saucepan, scald the cream over low heat (bring it to just below boiling point). Add the remaining salt and pepper and stir in the lemon juice. Simmer the cream sauce for 3 minutes, stirring constantly with a wooden spoon.

Remove the artichokes from the heat and transfer them to a warmed serving dish. Pour over the cream sauce and sprinkle with the nutmeg. Serve the

artichokes immediately.

Asparagus with Eggs

☆

This delicately-flavoured dish is easy and quick to make and is an elegant start to a dinner, or, accompanied by salad and brown bread and butter, a light snack lunch.

6 SERVINGS

3 lb. frozen asparagus, thawed and drained

3 hard-boiled eggs, shells removed and chopped

2 tablespoons finely chopped fresh parsley

½ teaspoon salt

¼ teaspoon freshly ground black pepper

6 oz. [¾ cup] butter, melted

2 tablespoons lemon juice

Cook the asparagus for 4 to 6 minutes according to the method indicated on page 2 (under Asparagus with Butter Sauce).

Meanwhile, using a fork, thoroughly blend the eggs, parsley, salt and black pepper in a medium-sized mixing bowl. Stirring constantly, add the melted butter, a little at a time. Continue stirring until the sauce is smooth, then stir in the lemon juice.

Drain the asparagus and transfer it to a large, heated serving dish. Pour over the sauce and serve the asparagus at once.

Aubergines Gratinées

  ① ① ⋈

This excellent vegetarian dish can be served either as a main course on its own, or as an accompaniment to meat or chicken.

4 SERVINGS

4 aubergines [eggplants], sliced and dégorged
3 oz. [¾ cup] flour
3 fl. oz. [⅜ cup] vegetable oil
5 oz. [1¼ cups] Parmesan cheese, grated
1 oz. [⅓ cup] dry white breadcrumbs
1 oz. [2 tablespoons] butter, cut into small pieces

SAUCE

1½ oz. [3 tablespoons] butter
1 small onion, finely chopped
3 tablespoons flour
14 oz. canned peeled tomatoes
1 teaspoon tomato purée
½ teaspoon dried basil
¼ teaspoon black pepper
½ teaspoon salt

To make the sauce, in a saucepan, melt the butter over moderate heat. When the foam subsides, add the onion and fry for 5 minutes or until it is soft. Stir in the flour and cook for 1 minute.

Strain the liquid from the tomatoes and stir it into the onion mixture. Add the tomatoes, tomato purée, basil, pepper and salt. Bring to the boil, stirring constantly. Reduce the heat to low, cover and simmer the sauce for 15 minutes.

Preheat the oven to moderate 350°F (Gas Mark 4, 180°C).

Dry the aubergine [eggplant] slices with kitchen paper towels. Dip the slices into the flour to coat. In a large frying-pan, heat half the oil over moderately

high heat. When the oil is hot, add the aubergine slices, a few at a time. Fry, turning occasionally with tongs, until they are well browned. Remove and drain on kitchen paper towels. Keep hot while you fry the remaining slices in the same way, adding more oil if necessary.

Pour a layer of the sauce into an oven-proof casserole. Sprinkle over some of the cheese, then put in a layer of aubergines [eggplants]. Continue making layers until all the ingredients are used up, finishing with a layer of sauce. Sprinkle over the remaining cheese and all the breadcrumbs. Dot with the butter. Bake in the oven for 25 minutes or until golden brown. Serve at once.

Caponata

☆ ① ① ⋈ ⋈ ⋈

A tangy vegetable dish, Caponata may be served as an appetizer to a dinner or as an extra-special accompaniment to cold roasted meat.

4-6 SERVINGS

4 small aubergines [eggplants], peeled, diced and dégorged
4 fl. oz. [½ cup] olive oil
4 celery stalks, thinly sliced
2 large onions, thinly sliced
4 oz. tomato purée diluted in 2 fl. oz. [¼ cup] water
1 tablespoon capers
2 oz. green olives, chopped
3 fl. oz. [⅜ cup] red wine vinegar
1 tablespoon sugar

Rinse the aubergines [eggplants] with cold water and pat them dry with kitchen paper towels.

In a large frying-pan, heat 3 fluid ounces [⅜ cup] of oil over moderate heat.

Versatile Aubergines Gratinées is delicious with meat or on its own.

Add the diced aubergines [eggplants] and cook for 8 to 10 minutes, or until they are soft and brown. Remove them from the pan and drain them in a colander. Dry them slightly on kitchen paper towels and set aside.

Pour the remaining oil into the pan and add the celery and onions. Cook for 8 minutes, or until they are lightly coloured. Pour in the tomato purée mixture and stir to coat the vegetables. Reduce the heat to low and simmer the mixture, covered, for 15 minutes.

Stir in the capers, olives, vinegar and sugar. Return the aubergines [eggplants] to the pan and coat with the sauce. Cook over low heat for 20 minutes.

Remove the caponata from the heat and transfer it to a serving dish. Chill in the refrigerator for at least 2 hours, or until you are ready to serve.

Imam Bayeldi

☆ ☆ ① ① ⋈ ⋈ ⋈

A classic Turkish dish of aubergines [eggplants] stuffed with tomatoes, raisins and onions, Imam Bayeldi means, literally, 'the priest has fainted'.

4-6 SERVINGS

4 aubergines [eggplants]
1½ teaspoons salt
2 oz. [¼ cup] butter
4 onions, thinly sliced
2 garlic cloves, crushed
6 large tomatoes, blanched, peeled, seeded and chopped
2 oz. [⅓ cup] raisins
1 teaspoon black pepper

½ teaspoon dried thyme
1 tablespoon chopped fresh parsley
10 fl. oz. [1¼ cups] olive oil

Halve the aubergines [eggplants] and hollow out four deep slits, ¼-inch wide, crosswise in each half, reserving the scooped out flesh. Sprinkle with 1 teaspoon of the salt and dégorge for 30 minutes. Drain the aubergines [eggplants] and set aside.

Meanwhile, in a large frying-pan, melt the butter over moderate heat. When the foam subsides, add the onions and garlic and cook them, stirring occasionally, for 5 to 7 minutes, or until they are soft and translucent but not brown.

Add the tomatoes, raisins, reserved aubergine [eggplant] flesh, the remaining salt, the pepper, thyme and parsley. Reduce the heat to low and simmer the mixture, stirring occasionally, for 10 to 12 minutes, or until it has pulped. Remove the pan from the heat and allow the mixture to cool.

Preheat the oven to cool 300°F (Gas Mark 2, 150°C).

When the mixture is cool, spoon it into the slits in the reserved aubergine [eggplant] halves. Spread the remaining mixture over the top of each half.

Place the aubergines [eggplants] in an ovenproof dish large enough to hold them in one layer. Spoon 1 tablespoon of olive oil over the top of each aubergine [eggplant] half, then pour the remaining oil carefully around them. The oil should come about one-quarter of the way up the sides of the aubergines [eggplants].

Bake the mixture for 1¾ hours, or until the aubergines [eggplants] are very soft and there is a slightly sticky residue on the bottom of the dish.

Remove the dish from the oven and cool to room temperature. Chill the aubergines [eggplants] in the refrigerator for 1 hour, or until they are very cold.

Remove the dish from the refrigerator, carefully transfer the aubergines [eggplants] to a serving dish and serve.

Guacamole

A piquant dish from Latin America, Guacamole is equally good as a dip or a dressing.

12 FLUID OUNCES [1½ CUPS]

3 medium-sized avocados
3 teaspoons lemon juice
2 teaspoons olive oil
½ teaspoon salt
½ teaspoon black pepper
½ teaspoon ground coriander
1 hard-boiled egg, finely chopped
½ small green pepper, white pith removed, seeded and chopped
1½ chillis, blanched and chopped
2 spring onions [scallions], chopped
1 tomato, blanched, peeled, seeded and chopped

Halve the avocados. Slice off the skins and cut out the stones. Discard the stones and skin. Place the flesh in a mixing bowl and mash it with a fork.

Add the lemon juice, oil, salt, pepper and coriander, and stir to blend. Still stirring, add the egg, green pepper, chillis, spring onions [scallions] and tomato. The dip should be fairly thick. It is best used immediately, but if it is to be kept, cover the bowl with foil and store in the refrigerator. Stir well before serving.

The perfect start to any festive meal – colourful Guacamole!

Harvard Beets

One of the most famous of all American vegetable dishes, Harvard Beets makes a delicious and unusual accompaniment to fried calf's or lamb's liver or tender boiled beef.

4 SERVINGS

2 oz. [¼ cup] sugar
1 teaspoon cornflour [cornstarch]
2 fl. oz. [¼ cup] vinegar
4 fl. oz. [½ cup] water
1 lb. cooked beetroots [beets],
   thinly sliced

In a small mixing bowl, combine the sugar and cornflour [cornstarch] and set the bowl aside.

In a medium-sized saucepan, heat the vinegar and water together over low heat. When the mixture is lukewarm, gradually add the sugar mixture, stirring constantly with a wooden spoon until it is completely absorbed. Bring the mixture to the boil and cook, stirring constantly, for 2 minutes, or until the sauce is fairly thick and smooth.

Add the beetroots [beets] to the pan and stir to baste well. Simmer the beetroots [beets] for 5 to 8 minutes, or until they are heated through.

Remove the pan from the heat and serve at once.

Broccoli Soufflé, filled with tiny new potatoes, makes a delicious vegetable accompaniment to roasts or fish.

Broccoli Soufflé

A tasty and attractive dish, Broccoli Soufflé may be filled with tiny, new boiled potatoes and served with almost any meat or fish dish.

6 SERVINGS

1½ oz. [3 tablespoons] butter
 1 oz. [¼ cup] plus 1 tablespoon flour
10 fl. oz. [1¼ cups] water
1½ teaspoons salt
1½ lb. broccoli, trimmed, washed
   and cut into small pieces
1 garlic clove
8 fl. oz. double cream [1 cup heavy
   cream]
4 eggs, separated and the yolks
   lightly beaten
¼ teaspoon black pepper
2 oz. [½ cup] Parmesan cheese,
   grated

Grease a 2-pint [1¼-quart] ring mould with 1 tablespoon of butter and lightly coat the mould with 1 tablespoon of flour. Knock out any excess flour and set the mould aside.

In a large saucepan bring the water, with 1 teaspoon salt, to the boil. Place the broccoli and garlic in the water, bring the water back to the boil, cover the pan and cook the broccoli over moderate heat for 15 minutes. Discard the garlic.

Drain the broccoli, chop it finely and set it aside in a large bowl.

Preheat the oven to moderate 350°F (Gas Mark 4, 180°C).

In a medium-sized saucepan melt the remaining butter over low heat. Stir in the remaining flour. Cook for 1 minute, stirring constantly. Slowly add the cream, stirring constantly with a wooden spoon. When the sauce is thick and smooth, stir in the broccoli. Remove the pan from the heat and stir in the beaten egg yolks, the remaining ½ teaspoon of salt and the pepper.

In a medium-sized mixing bowl, using a wire whisk, beat the egg whites until they form stiff peaks. With a metal spoon, carefully fold the egg whites into the broccoli mixture. Turn the mixture into the buttered mould. Stand the mould in a pan of boiling water and bake it in the oven for 35 to 40 minutes, or until the soufflé has risen and is set.

Remove the mould from the oven and loosen the soufflé with a knife. Place a serving platter, inverted, over the mould and reverse the two. The soufflé should slide out easily. Sprinkle over the Parmesan cheese and serve at once.

Carrot Cake

This unusual American Jewish cake is made with eggs, carrots and ground almonds. The finished cake has a moist consistency rather like cheesecake. Serve with tea or coffee as a morning or afternoon snack.

ONE 9-INCH CAKE

   1 teaspoon butter
   6 eggs, separated
   8 oz. [1 cup] sugar
12 oz. carrots, cooked and puréed
   1 tablespoon finely grated orange
     rind
   1 tablespoon brandy
12 oz. [2 cups] ground almonds

Preheat the oven to warm 325°F (Gas Mark 3, 170°C). With the teaspoon of butter, lightly grease a 9-inch loose-bottomed cake tin.

In a medium-sized bowl, beat the egg yolks with a wire whisk until they begin to thicken. Gradually add the sugar and continue beating until the mixture is thick and creamy. Add the carrot purée, orange rind, brandy and almonds and stir to mix thoroughly.

In a large bowl, beat the egg whites with a wire whisk or a rotary beater until they form stiff peaks. With a metal spoon or rubber spatula, carefully fold the egg whites into the carrot mixture.

Pour the mixture into the cake tin and bake in the centre of the oven for about 50 minutes, or until a skewer inserted into the centre of the cake comes out clean.

Remove the cake from the oven and leave it to cool in the tin for 15 minutes. Turn the cake out on to a wire rack to cool completely.

Serve cold.

Carrots and Onions with Raisins in Wine Sauce

A fascinating and exotic-tasting blend of vegetables and herbs, Carrots and Onions with Raisins in Wine Sauce makes a most impressive accompaniment to meat at a dinner party.

4 SERVINGS

2 oz. [¼ cup] butter
1 lb. carrots, scraped and cut into
   1-inch slices
8 oz. small white onions, peeled and
   left whole
4 oz. [⅔ cup] sultanas or seedless
   raisins

1 teaspoon salt
1 teaspoon black pepper
½ teaspoon cayenne pepper
1 teaspoon dried thyme
1 bay leaf
4 fl. oz. [½ cup] medium-dry white
   wine
2 fl. oz. double cream [¼ cup heavy
   cream]

In a large saucepan, melt the butter over moderate heat. When the foam subsides, add the carrots, onions and sultanas or raisins. Cook them, stirring constantly, for 4 minutes. Add the salt, pepper, cayenne, thyme and bay leaf to the pan. Pour in the wine, mixing well to blend. Cover the pan, reduce the heat to very low and simmer for 45 to 50 minutes, or until the carrots and onions are tender but still firm.

Remove the pan from the heat and remove and discard the bay leaf. Stir in the cream. Return the pan to very low heat for 1 to 2 minutes to warm the sauce slightly. Turn into a warmed serving dish and serve the mixture immediately.

Carrots and Onions with Raisins in Wine Sauce makes an interesting and 'different' vegetable accompaniment to plain meat dishes.

Pain de Chou Fleur
CAULIFLOWER LOAF

This beautifully elegant supper party dish makes a spectacular accompaniment to grilled [broiled] steak or to a roast. Served with a tossed mixed salad and brown bread, it is a complete and light spring luncheon in itself.

4-6 SERVINGS

2 medium-sized cauliflowers, broken into flowerets
1 tablespoon plus 1 teaspoon butter
1½ lb. potatoes, cooked and quartered
2 teaspoons salt
1 teaspoon white pepper
¼ teaspoon cayenne pepper
6 eggs
5 oz. [1¼ cups] Gruyère cheese, grated

Place the cauliflowers in a large saucepan and add enough water just to cover. Place the pan over moderately high heat and bring the water to the boil. Reduce the heat to moderate and cook the cauliflowers for 12 to 15 minutes or until the flowerets are very tender. Drain the flowerets in a colander and set aside.

Preheat the oven to moderate 350°F (Gas Mark 4, 180°C). Lightly grease a 4-pint [2½-quart] mould with the teaspoon of butter. Set aside.

Place the cauliflower, potatoes, the remaining butter, the salt, pepper and cayenne in a large mixing bowl. With a potato masher or fork, mash the ingredients together to form a purée. Add the eggs, one by one, beating well between each addition. Alternatively, purée the cauliflower and potatoes with the butter, seasoning and eggs in an electric blender.

Add 4½ ounces [1 cup plus 2 tablespoons] of the grated cheese and stir until it blends into the mixture.

Spoon the purée into the mould. Cover it tightly with aluminium foil and place the mould in a roasting tin one-third full of boiling water. Place the tin in the centre of the oven and bake the mixture for 1 hour.

Remove the roasting tin from the oven and remove the mould from the tin. Remove the aluminium foil. Place a heat-proof serving dish, inverted, over the top of the mould and turn the loaf out. Sprinkle the top of the loaf with the remaining grated cheese and put the dish

Walnut Cauliflower is warming, filling and so good to eat. Serve on its own or as an accompaniment.

back into the oven. Bake for a further 5 minutes to melt the cheese.

Remove the loaf from the oven and serve immediately.

Walnut Cauliflower

Cooked cauliflower covered in a creamy, mustard-flavoured walnut sauce, Walnut Cauliflower may be served as a vegetable accompaniment to plain meat dishes or as a vegetarian meal.

4-6 SERVINGS

1 oz. [2 tablespoons] butter
1 oz. [¼ cup] flour
12 fl. oz. [1½ cups] milk
6 fl. oz. single cream [¾ cup light cream]
1 egg, lightly beaten
2 fl. oz. [¼ cup] cider vinegar
2 tablespoons soft brown sugar
2 tablespoons prepared French mustard
4 oz. [⅔ cup] walnuts, coarsely chopped and toasted
1 medium-sized cauliflower, cooked until tender and kept hot

In a medium-sized saucepan, melt the butter over moderate heat. Remove the pan from the heat and, using a wooden spoon, stir in the flour to make a smooth paste. A little at a time, add the milk and cream, stirring constantly and being careful to avoid lumps. Add the egg, vinegar, sugar and mustard. Return the pan to low heat and cook, stirring constantly, for a further 2 to 3 minutes or until the sauce is thick and smooth. Do not allow the sauce to come to the boil or the egg will scramble. Stir in the walnuts and cook for a further 1 minute, stirring constantly.

Remove the pan from the heat. Place the cauliflower on a warmed serving dish and pour over the sauce.

Serve at once.

Celery with Almonds

The almonds in this celery dish give it a crisp and unusual texture. Celery with Almonds makes an excellent accompaniment to roast pork.

4 SERVINGS

2 medium-sized heads of celery, washed and the stalks cut into 2-inch lengths
2 oz. [¼ cup] butter
1 small onion, chopped
½ teaspoon salt
¼ teaspoon black pepper
1 tablespoon flour

8 fl. oz. single cream [1 cup light cream]
5 fl. oz. [⅝ cup] chicken stock
6 oz. [1½ cups] almonds, toasted and shredded

Prepare, parboil and drain the celery. In a medium-sized saucepan, melt the butter over moderate heat. Add the celery, onion, salt and pepper. Tightly cover the pan and reduce the heat to low. Cook for 15 minutes. Stir occasionally and, if the celery shows signs of sticking to the pan, add a little water.

Remove the pan from the heat. Sprinkle the flour into the pan and mix well. Gradually add the cream and stock, stirring constantly. Replace over moderate heat and cook, stirring constantly, until the sauce boils and thickens. Remove from the heat, stir in the almonds, and serve.

Endive Farcie
CHICORY [FRENCH OR BELGIAN ENDIVE]
LEAVES STUFFED WITH CREAM CHEESE

Endive Farcie is a delectable dish of chicory [French or Belgian endive] leaves stuffed with a mixture of cream cheese, cream, mustard and mixed nuts. The leaves are rolled and fastened, and served cold as an appetizer or as a snack with drinks.

6-8 SERVINGS

6 oz. cream cheese
3 fl. oz. double cream [⅜ cup heavy cream]
⅛ teaspoon cayenne pepper
¼ teaspoon salt
¼ teaspoon black pepper
½ teaspoon French mustard
1 teaspoon Worcestershire sauce
2½ oz. [½ cup] walnuts, finely chopped
2½ oz. [½ cup] hazelnuts, finely chopped
20 medium-sized to large chicory [French or Belgian endive] leaves, washed and shaken dry

In a medium-sized mixing bowl, mash the cream cheese with a fork until it is soft and smooth. Add the cream, cayenne, salt, pepper, mustard and Worcestershire sauce and beat well to blend the ingredients thoroughly. Stir in the nuts.

Lay the chicory [endive] leaves on a clean, flat surface. Put about 1 tablespoon of the cheese mixture on the base end of each leaf. Roll the leaves up and fasten each roll with a cocktail stick.

Arrange the stuffed leaves on a serving platter and place it in the refrigerator to chill for at least 30 minutes before serving.

41

Courgettes Gratinées à la Milanaise

COURGETTES [ZUCCHINI] BAKED WITH CHEESE

A light and subtle blend of tastes, Courgettes Gratinées à la Milanaise makes an excellent accompaniment to grilled [broiled] or roasted meats. Or serve with a tossed salad and brown bread and butter for an informal lunch.

4 SERVINGS

8 medium-sized courgettes [zucchini], trimmed, cleaned and blanched
2 oz. [¼ cup] butter
2 tablespoons olive oil
½ teaspoon salt
½ teaspoon white pepper
4 oz. [1 cup] Parmesan cheese, grated
1 oz. [2 tablespoons] melted butter

Using a sharp knife, cut the courgettes [zucchini] into ½-inch slices, crosswise, and dry them thoroughly on kitchen paper towels.

Preheat the oven to hot 425°F (Gas Mark 7, 220°C). Grease a large, oven-proof baking dish with a teaspoon of the butter.

In a large frying-pan, melt the remaining butter with the olive oil over moderate heat. When the foam subsides, add the courgette [zucchini] slices to the pan and cook them for 3 minutes, stirring occasionally to prevent them from sticking to the bottom of the pan. Add the salt and pepper. Remove the frying-pan from the heat.

Sprinkle the bottom of the baking dish with one-quarter of the grated cheese. Cover the cheese with a layer of courgette [zucchini] slices and on top of them spread a second layer of about 1 ounce [¼ cup] of grated cheese. Sprinkle 1 tablespoon of the melted butter over the cheese. Repeat the layers until all the courgettes [zucchini] and cheese have been used, then pour over the remaining melted butter.

Bake in the top part of the oven for 15 minutes, or until the courgettes [zucchini] are cooked and tender.

Serve immediately.

Zucchini Ripieni

STUFFED COURGETTES

These tasty stuffed courgettes [zucchini] are a regional speciality from Liguria in the north of Italy. Serve Zucchini Ripieni as a vegetable accompaniment to a plain meat dish, especially grilled [broiled] steaks or fried calf's liver.

6 SERVINGS

½ oz. dried mushrooms
12 medium-sized courgettes [zucchini], trimmed and cleaned
2 oz. [1 cup] fresh white breadcrumbs, soaked in 4 tablespoons milk
2 eggs, lightly beaten
½ teaspoon salt
1 teaspoon freshly ground black pepper
2 teaspoons finely chopped fresh oregano or 1 teaspoon dried oregano
6 oz. [1½ cups] Parmesan cheese, finely grated
2 oz. prosciutto, chopped
2 fl. oz. [¼ cup] olive oil

Place the dried mushrooms in a medium-sized mixing bowl, pour over enough water to cover and set aside to soak for 30 minutes. Drain the mushrooms, chop them finely and set aside.

Bring a large saucepan of salted water to the boil over high heat. Add the courgettes [zucchini] and boil for 7 to 8 minutes or until they are just tender when pierced with the point of a sharp knife. Remove the pan from the heat and drain the courgettes [zucchini] in a colander. With a sharp knife, slice the vegetables, lengthways, in half and, using a teaspoon, scoop out the flesh from each half, taking care not to break the skins. Set aside.

With your hands, squeeze any excess moisture out of the breadcrumbs and place them in a medium-sized mixing bowl. Add the reserved courgette [zucchini] flesh, the eggs, salt, pepper, oregano, half the cheese, the prosciutto and the reserved mushrooms. Using your hands or a wooden spoon, mix all the ingredients together until they are thoroughly combined.

Preheat the oven to fairly hot 400°F (Gas Mark 6, 200°C). Using a pastry brush, coat a shallow ovenproof casserole, large enough to take all the vegetables in one layer, with a little of the oil. Set the casserole aside.

Using a teaspoon, spoon a little of the stuffing into each courgette [zucchini] half and sprinkle the remaining cheese over the tops. Place the courgettes [zucchini] in the casserole and sprinkle with the remaining oil.

Place the casserole in the centre of the oven and cook for 15 minutes or until the cheese has melted and the courgettes [zucchini] are golden on top. Remove the casserole from the oven and transfer the courgettes [zucchini] to a warmed serving dish.

Serve immediately.

Fenouils à la Grecque

FENNELS GREEK-STYLE

An extremely aromatic dish, Fenouils à la Grecque is usually eaten — either hot or cold — as an hors d'oeuvre. If fennel is not available, artichoke hearts can be substituted.

4 SERVINGS

2 heads of fennel
4 tablespoons olive oil
8 oz. small white onions, peeled and left whole
1 teaspoon salt
½ teaspoon white pepper
½ teaspoon cayenne pepper
½ teaspoon ground coriander
½ teaspoon finely chopped fresh thyme or ¼ teaspoon dried thyme
1 bay leaf
2 tablespoons tomato purée
3 fl. oz. [⅜ cup] dry white wine
2 oz. [⅓ cup] sultanas or raisins

Wash and trim the fennel and discard any withered outer leaves. Cut the heads into quarters and set side.

In a large frying-pan, heat the olive oil over moderate heat. When the oil is hot, add the fennel pieces and small onions. Fry them, stirring occasionally, for 4 to 5 minutes. Add the salt, pepper, cayenne, coriander, thyme, bay leaf and tomato purée to the pan and mix to blend thoroughly.

Add the wine, cover the pan and reduce the heat to very low. Simmer for 30 minutes, or until the vegetables are tender. Halfway through the cooking period, add the sultanas or raisins.

When the vegetables are cooked, remove the pan from the heat and remove and discard the bay leaf.

Serve at once, if you are serving the dish hot.

Jerusalem Artichoke Soufflé

This delicious and unusual soufflé can be served as a light lunch dish with lots of melba toast or crusty bread and butter, or on its own as a first course for a lunch or dinner party.

4-6 SERVINGS

2 oz. [¼ cup] plus 1 teaspoon butter
2 oz. [½ cup] flour
10 fl. oz. [1¼ cups] milk
½ teaspoon salt

Fenouils à la Grecque is usually eaten as an aromatic hors d'oeuvre.

¼ teaspoon freshly ground black
  pepper
⅛ teaspoon cayenne pepper
¼ teaspoon finely chopped fresh
  oregano or ⅛ teaspoon dried
  oregano
2 oz. [½ cup] Parmesan cheese,
  grated
8 oz. Jerusalem artichokes, peeled,
  simmered for about 30 minutes or
  until tender and drained
2 tablespoons double [heavy] cream
4 egg yolks
5 egg whites

Preheat the oven to fairly hot 375°F (Gas Mark 5, 190°C).

Using 1 teaspoon of the butter, grease a 3-pint [1½-quart] soufflé dish. Tie a strip of greaseproof or waxed paper around the rim of the soufflé dish so that it projects about 2 inches over the top. Set the soufflé dish aside.

In a large, heavy saucepan, melt the remaining butter over moderate heat. Remove the pan from the heat and, with a wooden spoon, stir in the flour to make a smooth paste. Gradually stir in the milk, being careful to avoid lumps.

Return the pan to the heat and cook the sauce for 2 to 3 minutes, stirring constantly, or until it becomes very thick and smooth.

Remove the pan from the heat. Stir in the salt, pepper, cayenne, oregano and cheese. Set aside to cool slightly.

Meanwhile, place a fine strainer over a medium-sized mixing bowl. Using the

back of a wooden spoon, rub the cooked artichokes through the strainer to make a purée.

Stir the puréed artichokes and the cream into the sauce mixture. Stir in the egg yolks and combine the mixture thoroughly. Set aside.

In a medium-sized mixing bowl, beat the egg whites with a wire whisk or rotary beater until they form stiff peaks.

Using a metal spoon, carefully fold the egg whites into the artichoke mixture.

Spoon the mixture into the prepared soufflé dish. Place the dish in the centre of the oven and bake for 35 to 40 minutes, or until the soufflé has risen and is golden brown on top.

Remove the dish from the oven. Quickly remove and discard the paper collar.

Serve the soufflé immediately.

Mushrooms Baked with Cream and Sherry

This unusual dinner party hors d'oeuvre is a luscious concoction of mushrooms flavoured with cream and sherry.

4 SERVINGS

1 oz. [2 tablespoons] butter
1 teaspoon lemon juice
1 teaspoon salt
3 slices of buttered toast, cut about ½ inch thick and with crusts removed
1 lb. mushrooms, wiped clean and with the stems removed
½ teaspoon black pepper
4 fl. oz. double cream [½ cup heavy cream]
1 tablespoon sherry

Preheat the oven to fairly hot 375°F (Gas Mark 5, 190°C).

In a small mixing bowl, combine the butter with ½ teaspoon lemon juice and ½ teaspoon salt, beating with a wooden spoon until the mixture becomes light and creamy.

Coat the bottom and sides of a deep, round ovenproof dish with the mixture and arrange the toast slices on the bottom. Pile the mushroom caps, pyramid-style, on the toast. Season the pyramid with the remaining salt, pepper and lemon juice and cover it with 3

Mushrooms Baked with Cream and Sherry is an unusual hors d'oeuvre.

fluid ounces [⅜ cup] of cream.

Cover the dish and bake in the oven for 15 to 20 minutes. Five minutes before the end of the cooking period, add the remaining cream to the mixture.

Remove the dish from the oven and sprinkle the mushrooms with the sherry.

Onions in Sweet and Sour Sauce

An adaptation of a famous Italian recipe, Onions in Sweet and Sour Sauce may be eaten hot as a vegetable accompaniment, or cold as part of a cold buffet or hors d'oeuvre.

6 SERVINGS

3 fl. oz. [⅜ cup] olive oil
1 lb. pickling (pearl) onions, peeled and blanched for 5 minutes
2 fl. oz. [¼ cup] malt vinegar
2 tablespoons soft brown sugar
3 oz. [½ cup] walnuts, chopped
3 oz. [½ cup] raisins (optional)

In a medium-sized saucepan, heat the oil over moderate heat. When the oil is hot, add the onions and cook, stirring occasionally, for 8 to 10 minutes, or until they are lightly browned. With a slotted spoon,

transfer the onions to a plate.

Add the vinegar and sugar to the pan and cook, stirring frequently, for 5 minutes, or until the sugar has dissolved and the mixture is hot. Return the onions to the pan and cook for 3 minutes, basting frequently.

Stir in the walnuts and raisins, if you are using them, and cook for 2 minutes.

Remove the pan from the heat and transfer the onion mixture to a warmed serving dish. Serve immediately if you are serving the dish hot. Or set aside to cool, if you are serving cold.

Stuffed Green Peppers

Peppers stuffed with scrambled eggs, onion and cheese, Stuffed Green Peppers make a light and colourful first course or a vegetable accompaniment to a main course. Serve them hot on their own or cold with French dressing with chopped parsley.

6 SERVINGS

1 teaspoon olive oil
6 medium-sized green peppers, wiped clean
4 eggs
½ teaspoon salt
½ teaspoon black pepper
2 teaspoons flour
2 tablespoons milk
1 large onion, finely chopped

1 garlic clove, crushed
2 oz. [½ cup] Parmesan cheese, grated
2 tablespoons chopped fresh parsley
2 egg yolks
2 egg whites, stiffly beaten

With the teaspoon of olive oil, lightly grease a medium-sized baking dish and set it aside.

With a sharp knife, slice off a 1-inch strip from the wider end of each pepper. Chop each pepper strip into small dice. Carefully remove and discard the white pith and seeds from the inside of each pepper. Set aside.

Half-fill a large saucepan with water and bring it to the boil over moderately high heat. Add the peppers and blanch them for 5 minutes. Remove the saucepan from the heat. Using a slotted spoon, remove the peppers from the water and pat them dry with kitchen paper towels. Set aside.

Preheat the oven to moderate 350°F (Gas Mark 4, 180°C).

In a medium-sized heatproof mixing bowl, set over a saucepan half-filled with hot water, combine the eggs, salt, pepper, flour and milk. Beating constantly with a wire whisk or rotary beater, cook the mixture over low heat until it thickens.

Remove the pan from the heat and stir in the onion, garlic, chopped pepper, cheese and parsley. When these are thoroughly incorporated, fold in the egg yolks and then the egg whites with a metal spoon.

Spoon equal quantities of the egg mixture into each pepper.

Stand the peppers upright in the prepared baking dish and place the dish in the centre of the oven. Bake for 20 to 25 minutes or until the tops are golden brown.

Remove the dish from the oven and transfer the peppers to a warmed serving dish. Either serve them immediately or leave them to cool.

Peperonata

Peperonata is equally good hot or cold and will keep for several days if stored in a screw-top jar.

4-6 SERVINGS

1 oz. [2 tablespoons] butter
2 tablespoons olive oil
1 large onion, thinly sliced
1 garlic clove, crushed
1 lb. red peppers, white pith removed, seeded and cut into strips

1 lb. tomatoes, blanched, peeled and chopped
½ teaspoon salt
¼ teaspoon black pepper
1 bay leaf

In a large saucepan, heat the butter with the oil over moderate heat. When the foam subsides, add the onion and garlic and fry, stirring occasionally, for 5 to 7 minutes or until the onion is soft and translucent but not brown.

Add the red peppers. Cover, reduce the heat to low and cook for 15 minutes. Add the tomatoes, salt, pepper and bay leaf and simmer for 25 minutes.

Remove the pan from the heat and remove and discard the bay leaf. Serve at once, if you are serving hot.

Petits Pois à la Française

One of the classic vegetable dishes of French cuisine, Petits Pois à la Française is easy both to prepare and to eat! Serve it with

Petits Pois à la Française is one of the classics of French cuisine.

omelets, or with grilled [broiled] chops or steaks.

4-6 SERVINGS

1½ lb. small fresh garden peas, weighed after shelling or 1½ lb. frozen petits pois
1 teaspoon salt
½ teaspoon black pepper
1 teaspoon sugar
1 onion, thinly sliced
4 lettuce leaves, washed, shaken dry and shredded
1 tablespoon butter blended into a paste with 1 tablespoon flour

Place the peas, salt, pepper, sugar, onion and lettuce in a large saucepan. Pour over enough hot water to cover the peas and set the pan over moderately high heat. Bring the water to the boil.

Reduce the heat to very low, cover the pan and simmer the pea mixture for 20 to 30 minutes or until the onion is soft and translucent and the peas are very tender. Stir in the butter mixture, a little at a time, stirring constantly. Simmer the mixture for 2 minutes or until it has thickened.

Remove the pan from the heat. Spoon the mixture into a warmed serving dish and serve immediately.

Pommes de Terre Galette

A golden, crisp potato cake, Pommes de Terre Galette is excellent served with grilled [broiled] fish or meat.

4 SERVINGS

2 lb. potatoes, peeled and cooked
1 small onion, finely chopped
2 teaspoons salt
¼ teaspoon black pepper
1 tablespoon chopped fresh parsley
2 oz. [¼ cup] butter, softened
2 eggs, lightly beaten
½ teaspoon paprika

Preheat the oven to fairly hot 375°F (Gas Mark 5, 190°C).

With a potato masher or fork, mash the potatoes and place them in a medium-sized mixing bowl. Add the onion, salt, pepper and parsley and mix well.

Beat in 1½ ounces [3 tablespoons] of the butter and the eggs and stir until the ingredients are well blended.

Using the remaining butter, generously grease a medium-sized baking dish. Spoon the mixture into the dish, flattening the top with a palette knife. Sprinkle over the paprika.

Place the dish in the oven and bake the mixture for 20 to 30 minutes or until it is golden brown and crisp.

Remove the dish from the oven and cut the galette into wedges. Serve immediately.

Potatoes Country-Style

This sustaining mixture of fried potato cubes, onion, bread croûtons and eggs, makes a filling accompaniment to lamb chops or ham. Or, served with lots of cold beer and crusty bread, it may be served as a snack lunch.

4-6 SERVINGS

1½ lb. potatoes, weighed after peeling
2 teaspoons salt
2 oz. [¼ cup] butter
2 medium-sized onions, finely chopped
1 garlic clove, crushed
2 thick slices day-old white bread, crusts removed and cut into cubes
3 eggs
3 fl. oz. [⅜ cup] milk
½ teaspoon black pepper
¼ teaspoon dried thyme
1 tablespoon chopped fresh parsley

Place the potatoes in a large saucepan and pour over enough water just to cover. Add 1 teaspoon of the salt and place the pan over high heat. Bring the water to the

boil, reduce the heat to moderate and cook the potatoes for 8 minutes. Remove the pan from the heat and drain the potatoes. Set aside to cool slightly.

When the potatoes are cool enough to handle, transfer them to a chopping board. With a sharp knife, cut them into cubes and set aside.

Meanwhile, in a large, deep frying-pan, melt the butter over moderate heat. When the foam subsides, add the onions, garlic and bread cubes and cook, stirring occasionally, for 8 to 10 minutes or until the onions are golden brown.

Add the potato cubes to the pan and cook them, turning occasionally, for 5 to 8 minutes or until the potatoes are tender when pierced with the point of a sharp knife.

Meanwhile, in a small mixing bowl, beat the eggs, milk, the remaining salt, the pepper and thyme together until they are well blended.

Pour the egg mixture over the potato mixture and cook, stirring and turning constantly, for 3 minutes or until the eggs are cooked and the mixture is still moist.

Remove the pan from the heat and transfer the mixture to a warmed serving dish. Sprinkle over the parsley and serve at once.

Duchess Potatoes

This elegant potato purée can be piped around a meat entrée and served as it is, or it can be browned in the oven. It makes an excellent accompaniment to roast meats or steaks.

4-6 SERVINGS

1 lb. potatoes, thickly sliced
2 teaspoons salt
1 teaspoon vegetable oil
2 oz. [¼ cup] butter, softened
2 egg yolks
1 teaspoon white pepper
½ teaspoon grated nutmeg

Place the potatoes in a saucepan. Pour over enough water to cover the potatoes and add 1 teaspoon of the salt. Bring the water to the boil over high heat. Reduce the heat to low, cover the pan and simmer for 20 to 25 minutes, or until the potatoes are soft. Drain well.

Preheat the oven to fairly hot 400°F (Gas Mark 6, 200°C). With the vegetable oil, grease a baking sheet. Set it aside.

With a potato masher, mash the

potatoes until they are completely smooth. Add the butter, egg yolks, pepper, nutmeg and the remaining salt to the purée and mix well.

If you wish to pipe the purée into decorative shapes, fill a forcing bag with the mixture. Pipe the potato on to the baking sheet in the shapes you wish. Place the sheet in the centre of the oven and bake for 10 minutes, or until the potato purée is golden-brown. Remove

A filling mixture of potato cubes, onion, croûtons and eggs, that's Potatoes Country-Style.

the purée from the sheet and serve.

Potatoes Provençal-Style

This rustic, hearty dish of potatoes cooked in oil, garlic and anchovies is an excellent accompaniment to stews and casseroles.

4 SERVINGS

2 fl. oz. [¼ cup] olive oil

2 garlic cloves, crushed
2 lb. potatoes, parboiled in their skins for 10 minutes
½ teaspoon salt
¼ teaspoon black pepper
6 anchovy fillets, halved
1 tablespoon chopped fresh parsley

In a large frying-pan, heat the oil over moderate heat. When the oil is hot, add the garlic and cook, stirring constantly, for 3 minutes.

Peel the potatoes and cut them into ½-inch slices. Add the potatoes to the pan, sprinkle over the salt and pepper and cook them, turning once, for 10 to 12 minutes or until they are golden brown.

Just before serving, add the anchovy fillets and cook for a further 2 minutes.

Using a slotted spoon, transfer the potatoes to a warmed serving dish. Sprinkle with the parsley and serve.

Dulma

STUFFED AUBERGINES [EGGPLANTS],
COURGETTES [ZUCCHINI] AND TOMATOES

*A colourful Middle Eastern dish of mixed
vegetables stuffed with a tasty mixture of
lamb and rice, Dulma may be served with
saffron rice and salad.*

6 SERVINGS

4 small aubergines [eggplants]
2 teaspoons salt
6 small courgettes [zucchini]
6 large tomatoes
2 tablespoons olive oil
1 large onion, finely chopped
2 garlic cloves, crushed
1½ lb. minced [ground] lamb
6 tablespoons cooked rice
3 tablespoons chopped fresh parsley
2 tablespoons coriander seeds,
  crushed
½ teaspoon ground cumin
1 teaspoon turmeric
½ teaspoon black pepper
2 eggs
1 oz. [2 tablespoons] melted butter

With a small, sharp knife, score the skin

*Exotic Dulma makes an excitingly
different lunch for special guests.*

of the aubergines [eggplants] and cut
them in half, lengthways. Sprinkle the
halves with 1 teaspoon of salt and leave
them to dégorge on kitchen paper towels
for 30 minutes.

Wash the courgettes [zucchini] under
cold running water and dry them
thoroughly on kitchen paper towels. Cut
about ½-inch off both ends of each
courgette [zucchini]. With a teaspoon or
apple corer, carefully scoop out the
centre from each courgette [zucchini].
Discard the centre.

Cut the tops off the tomatoes and
hollow out the centres. Discard the
centres.

Wipe the moisture from the aubergines
[eggplants] with kitchen paper towels.
With a spoon, hollow out the centres,
leaving a ½-inch shell. Discard the centres.

Preheat the oven to moderate 350°F
(Gas Mark 4, 180°C).

In a large frying-pan, heat the oil over
moderate heat. When the oil is hot, add
the onion and garlic and fry for 8 to 10

minutes, or until the onion is browned.

Stir in the lamb and cook, stirring
occasionally, for 10 minutes, or until the
meat loses its pinkness.

Remove the pan from the heat and turn
the mixture into a large mixing bowl.

Add the rice, parsley, coriander, cumin,
turmeric, pepper and the remaining salt.
With a wooden spoon, stir the eggs into
the mixture. Beat the mixture vigorously
until it is well blended.

Spoon the mixture into the courgettes
[zucchini], tomatoes and aubergines [egg-
plants]. Replace the tomato lids.

Place the stuffed vegetables in a shallow
ovenproof dish. Spoon the melted butter
over the stuffed vegetables and place the
dish in the oven.

Bake for 45 to 50 minutes, or until the
vegetables are tender.

Remove the dish from the oven and
serve at once.

Fried Mixed Vegetables

*Fried Mixed Vegetables is a classic and
very popular Chinese dish, which may be*

48

served as part of a Chinese meal, or on its own as a vegetarian lunch or dinner.

2-4 SERVINGS

3 tablespoons vegetable oil
1 garlic clove, crushed
1-inch piece fresh root ginger, peeled and sliced
½ teaspoon salt
¼ teaspoon white pepper
2 carrots, scraped and thinly sliced
1 small green pepper, white pith removed, and shredded
1 very small cauliflower, trimmed washed and broken into flowerets
2 oz. bean sprouts, washed and shaken dry
5 fl. oz. [⅝ cup] chicken stock
2 teaspoons soy sauce
1 teaspoon soft brown sugar

In a large frying-pan, heat the oil over moderate heat. When it is hot, add the garlic, ginger, salt and pepper. Fry, stirring constantly, for 1 minute. Add the carrots and fry for a further minute, still stirring. Add the green pepper and cauliflower and stir-fry for 3 minutes. Add the bean sprouts and fry, stirring, for a further 1 minute. Stir in the stock, soy sauce and sugar. Cover the pan and cook for a further 4 minutes.

Remove the pan from the heat. Turn the vegetables into a warmed serving dish and serve immediately.

Légumes Nouveaux Flambés
MIXED FRESH VEGETABLES WITH BRANDY

Légumes Nouveaux Flambés (pictured on page 1) is a delicious way of cooking ordinary vegetables. Serve with braised lamb or pork chops.

8 SERVINGS

3 oz. [⅜ cup] butter
2 lb. carrots, scraped and cut into 1-inch lengths
1 lb. turnips, peeled and chopped
1 lb. small white onions, peeled
1 teaspoon salt
1 teaspoon black pepper
2 tablespoons soft brown sugar
3 fl. oz. [⅜ cup] brandy
2 tablespoons chopped fresh parsley

In a large frying-pan, melt the butter over moderate heat. When the foam subsides, add the carrots, turnips and onions and coat them thoroughly with the butter. Add the salt, pepper and brown sugar, and stir to blend. Reduce the heat to low, cover the pan and cook the vegetables for 35 minutes, basting occasionally.

In a small saucepan, gently heat the brandy over low heat until it is hot but not boiling. Remove the pan from the heat and ignite the brandy with a match. While it is still flaming, pour it into the frying-pan. When the flames die down, re-cover the pan and cook the mixture for a further 10 minutes, or until the vegetables are tender but still firm.

Remove the pan from the heat and transfer the mixture to a warmed serving dish. Sprinkle over the chopped parsley and serve at once.

Vegetable Paella

A colourful version of a Spanish national dish, Vegetable Paella is delicious.

4-6 SERVINGS

4 fl. oz. [½ cup] olive oil
2 large onions, thinly sliced
2 garlic cloves, crushed
1 large red pepper, white pith removed, seeded and sliced
12 oz. [2 cups] long-grain rice, washed, soaked in cold water for 30 minutes and drained
1 pint [2½ cups] vegetable stock
4 large tomatoes, blanched, peeled, seeded and chopped

This Chinese dish of Fried Mixed Vegetables is easy and quick to cook.

3 oz. frozen petits pois
2 celery stalks, chopped
18 black olives, halved and stoned
1 teaspoon salt
1 teaspoon black pepper
¼ teaspoon crushed saffron threads dissolved in 2 teaspoons hot water
2 oz. [½ cup] slivered almonds

In a saucepan, heat the oil over moderate heat. When the oil is hot, add the onions, garlic and red pepper. Cook, stirring occasionally, for 5 to 7 minutes or until the onions are soft and translucent but not brown Stir in the rice, coating it well with the oil, and continue cooking, stirring occasionally, for 5 minutes. Pour in the stock and increase the heat to high. Bring the liquid to the boil. Reduce the heat to low and stir in the tomatoes, petits pois, celery, olives, salt, pepper and saffron. Cover and simmer the mixture for 35 minutes or until the rice is tender.

Remove the pan from the heat and turn the paella into a warmed dish. Sprinkle over the almonds and serve.

Boston Baked Beans

Flavoured with molasses and baked to a dark, rich brown, Boston Baked Beans is a traditional American dish. In colonial New England, this nourishing combination of beans, salt pork and molasses was often baked in the oven with the week's bread and then eaten with thick slices of the steaming hot, brown bread. Today, Boston Baked Beans are usually served with roast pork or ham.

6-8 SERVINGS

8 oz. salt pork
2 lb. dried haricot, pea or kidney
  beans, washed, soaked in cold
  water overnight and drained
2 teaspoons salt
1 large onion
3 oz. [½ cup] soft brown sugar
6 tablespoons molasses or black
  treacle
3 teaspoons dry mustard
1 teaspoon black pepper

Put the salt pork in a large bowl. Add cold water to cover. Soak the salt pork for 3 hours and drain well.

Place the beans in a saucepan and add enough cold water to cover. Add 1 teaspoon of salt. Bring the water to the boil over high heat. Boil the beans for 2 minutes. Remove the pan from the heat and let the beans soak in the water for 1 hour.

Return the pan to the heat and bring the beans to the boil again. Reduce the heat to very low, partially cover the pan and slowly simmer the beans for 30 minutes. Drain the beans and discard the liquid.

Preheat the oven to very cool 250°F (Gas Mark ½, 130°C).

Place the onion in the bottom of a flameproof casserole. Add a layer of the cooked, drained beans to the casserole. Add another layer of beans and finish with a layer of salt pork.

Thickly slice the drained salt pork and cut each slice into small chunks. Arrange a layer of salt pork over the beans in the casserole. Add another layer of beans and finish with a layer of salt pork.

In a small mixing bowl, with a wooden spoon, mix together the brown sugar, molasses or treacle, mustard, black pepper and the remaining 1 teaspoon of salt. Spoon the mixture over the beans and pork. Add enough boiling water to cover the beans.

Cover the casserole and place it in the oven. Bake for 5 hours, adding boiling water from time to time so that the beans are always just covered.

Remove the lid of the casserole and bake uncovered for 45 minutes. Serve straight from the casserole.

Red Cabbage and Bacon Casserole

A hearty winter dish from Czechoslovakia, Red Cabbage and Bacon Casserole makes an economical and filling special lunch or supper. Accompany the casserole with fresh rye bread and butter and some well-chilled lager.

4 SERVINGS

1½ tablespoons vegetable oil
1 large onion, finely sliced
6 streaky bacon slices, chopped
1 large cooking apple, peeled, cored
  and sliced
2 large potatoes, sliced
1 medium-sized red cabbage,
  washed, coarse outer leaves
  removed and shredded
1½ teaspoons caraway seeds
2 tablespoons lemon juice
1 tablespoon wine vinegar
1 teaspoon salt
½ teaspoon black pepper
10 fl. oz. [1¼ cups] chicken stock
1 tablespoon soft brown sugar

In a large flameproof casserole, heat the oil over moderate heat. Add the onion and cook, stirring occasionally, for 8 minutes, or until it is browned. Add the bacon to the pan and, stirring occasionally, cook until the pieces become brown.

Preheat the oven to moderate 350°F (Gas Mark 4, 180°C).

Stir the apple, potatoes, red cabbage, caraway seeds, lemon juice, vinegar, salt, pepper, stock and brown sugar into the pan and bring the liquid to the boil, stirring occasionally.

Cover the casserole and transfer it to the oven. Braise for 2 hours, or until the cabbage is very tender.

Remove from the oven and serve.

Spinach Ring

A tempting cold dish, Spinach Ring may be served on its own or as an edible container for egg mayonnaise, shrimps in cream sauce or ham in sour cream. The filled Spinach Ring makes an attractive hors d'oeuvre or a light luncheon or buffet dish. It is important to squeeze as much moisture as possible from the spinach when draining it.

4-6 SERVINGS

1½ lb. spinach, cooked, drained and
  chopped
½ cucumber, finely chopped
6 spring onions [scallions], chopped
½ teaspoon dried marjoram
¼ teaspoon salt

½ teaspoon black pepper
¼ teaspoon dry mustard
½ oz. gelatine, dissolved in 3
  tablespoons hot water
14 fl. oz. [1¾ cups] chicken stock
2 tablespoons cider vinegar

In a large mixing bowl, combine the spinach, cucumber, spring onions [scallions], marjoram, salt, pepper and mustard. Rinse a 2-pint [1¼-quart] ring mould with cold water. Spoon the spinach mixture into the prepared mould and mix thoroughly.

Pour the dissolved gelatine, stock and vinegar into the bowl and stir well. Pour the mixture into the ring mould.

Chill the ring mould in the refrigerator for 4 hours or until the mixture has set. Remove the ring mould from the refrigerator. Quickly dip the bottom of the mould into hot water, place a chilled serving dish over the top and invert the two, giving the mould a sharp shake. The spinach ring should slide out easily.

Serve immediately.

Sweetcorn Bake

Serve as a sustaining accompaniment to steaks or chops or with crusty bread and salad as a light lunch or supper dish.

4-6 SERVINGS

1 oz. [2 tablespoons] butter
1½ lb. sweetcorn kernels
14 oz. canned peeled tomatoes
5 oz. tomato purée
2 tablespoons flour
2 tablespoons treacle or molasses
½ teaspoon salt
1 teaspoon black pepper
½ teaspoon cayenne pepper
½ teaspoon dry mustard
4 oz. [1 cup] Cheddar cheese, grated

Preheat the oven to moderate 350°F (Gas Mark 4, 180°C). With a little butter, lightly grease a medium-sized baking dish and set aside.

In a mixing bowl, combine the sweetcorn, tomatoes with the can juice, tomato purée, flour, treacle or molasses, salt, pepper, cayenne and mustard and beat well. Spoon the mixture into the dish.

Sprinkle over the cheese. Cut the remaining butter into small pieces and dot them over the cheese. Place the dish in the oven and bake for 30 minutes or until the top of the mixture is brown.

Remove from the oven and serve.

Serve Boston Baked Beans with brown bread for a super supper.

Artichoke Heart Salad

This delicately flavoured hors d'oeuvre may be served with thinly sliced brown bread and butter.

4 SERVINGS

12 canned artichoke hearts, drained and quartered
2 shallots, finely chopped
½ teaspoon finely grated lemon rind
6 small new potatoes, scrubbed, cooked and quartered
DRESSING
3 fl. oz. [⅜ cup] olive oil
1 tablespoon white wine vinegar
1 tablespoon lemon juice
½ teaspoon salt
½ teaspoon black pepper
½ teaspoon chopped fresh tarragon or ¼ teaspoon dried tarragon
½ teaspoon chopped fresh basil or ¼ teaspoon dried basil
GARNISH
2 small tomatoes, quartered
8 black olives, halved and stoned

In a medium-sized glass serving bowl, combine the artichoke hearts, shallots, lemon rind and potatoes. Set aside.

In a small mixing bowl, combine all the dressing ingredients and beat well with a fork until they are thoroughly combined. Alternatively, place all the dressing ingredients in a small screw-top jar, screw on the lid and shake vigorously until they are thoroughly combined.

Pour the dressing over the artichoke heart mixture and toss well with two large spoons. Garnish with the tomatoes and olives.

Either serve the salad immediately or cover and chill in the refrigerator until required.

Bean Sprout Salad

This fresh, crunchy salad is ideal to serve with or after grilled [broiled] fish or chicken, or with other salads.

4 SERVINGS

1 lb. fresh or canned and drained bean sprouts
2 oz. canned pimiento, chopped

1 pickled cucumber, chopped
1 tablespoon finely chopped fresh chives
DRESSING
2 tablespoons olive oil
1 tablespoon wine vinegar
½ teaspoon prepared mustard
2 teaspoons soy sauce
½ teaspoon sugar
½ teaspoon salt

Put the bean sprouts in a salad bowl with the pimiento, pickled cucumber and chives.

Mix all the ingredients for the dressing together, making sure the salt and sugar are dissolved. Pour the dressing over the salad. Toss the salad well and put in a refrigerator or a cool place for 1 hour before serving.

Beetroot and Orange Salad

This is a delicious salad of contrasting flavours, textures and colours.

4 SERVINGS

6 beetroots [beets], cooked
2 large oranges
2 bunches watercress
DRESSING
4 tablespoons olive oil
1½ tablespoons wine vinegar
1 teaspoon prepared mustard
¼ teaspoon dried tarragon
½ teaspoon salt
½ teaspoon sugar

Peel and slice the beetroots [beets] into rounds. Grate the rind of 1 orange and set aside. Peel the oranges, removing the white pith, and slice them into rounds.

Wash the watercress and cut off the stalks. Arrange the watercress on a shallow serving dish.

Arrange the beetroot [beet] and orange slices alternately, overlapping, on the bed of watercress.

Mix all the dressing ingredients in a cup and add the reserved orange rind.

Spoon the dressing over the overlapping slices just before serving.

Coleslaw with Caraway

Caraway seeds provide the interesting variation in this crisp coleslaw salad. It is a perfect accompaniment to cold meat and cold roast chicken.

Beetroot and Orange Salad provides an unusual blend of taste and texture.

8 SERVINGS

1 large white cabbage, coarse outer leaves removed, washed, cored and shredded
1 medium-sized onion, finely chopped
½ green pepper, white pith removed, seeded and finely chopped
½ teaspoon lemon juice
1 tablespoon caraway seeds

DRESSING

6 fl. oz. double cream [¾ cup heavy cream]
3 fl. oz. [⅜ cup] sour cream
1 tablespoon prepared French mustard
3 tablespoons lemon juice
1 tablespoon sugar
½ teaspoon salt
¼ teaspoon white pepper

Arrange the shredded cabbage in a large serving dish and sprinkle with the onion, green pepper and lemon juice. Set aside.

In a medium-sized mixing bowl, combine the double [heavy] cream, sour cream, mustard and lemon juice, beating vigorously with a wooden spoon until the ingredients are thoroughly blended. Add the sugar, salt and white pepper and mix well.

Pour the dressing over the shredded

Crunchy, nutritious Coleslaw with Caraway tastes even better than it looks. Serve with cold meat or pâté.

cabbage and add the caraway seeds to the mixture. Using two large spoons or forks, toss the cabbage mixture until it is completely saturated with dressing. Chill in the refrigerator for at least 1 hour and serve cold.

Cucumber and Yogurt Salad

Cucumber and Yogurt Salad is both crunchy and creamy. Serve it as an accompaniment to cold meat dishes or with hot dishes such as curries or goulasches.

6 SERVINGS

1 cucumber, peeled and finely chopped
2 tablespoons malt vinegar
1 teaspoon sugar
6 spring onions [scallions], trimmed and finely chopped
1 green pepper, white pith removed, seeded and finely chopped
8 fl. oz. [1 cup] yogurt
2 fl. oz. [¼ cup] sour cream
1 teaspoon salt

½ teaspoon black pepper
3 teaspoons chopped fresh dill or 1½ teaspoons dried dill
1 round [Boston] lettuce, outer leaves removed, washed and separated into leaves

Place the cucumber in a small mixing bowl and add the vinegar and sugar. Set aside for 10 minutes to dégorge.

Place the cucumber in a wire strainer held over a small mixing bowl. With the back of a wooden spoon, gently press the cucumber until most of the liquid is extracted. Discard the liquid.

Place the cucumber in a medium-sized mixing bowl and add the spring onions [scallions] and green pepper. Mix them together with the wooden spoon and set aside.

In another medium-sized mixing bowl, mix the yogurt, sour cream, salt, pepper and two-thirds of the dill. Pour the yogurt mixture over the cucumber mixture and toss them together with two large spoons until all the ingredients are thoroughly coated.

Arrange the lettuce leaves around the edges of a large serving platter and spoon the yogurt and cucumber mixture into the centre. Sprinkle the remaining dill over the mixture and serve immediately.

Danish Blue Salad

This fresh, colourful cheese salad may be served with cold ham, or on its own as a light snack.

2 SERVINGS

2 oz. Danish blue cheese, cut into small pieces
2 oz. Cheddar cheese, cut into small pieces
1 medium-sized red pepper, white pith removed, seeded and thinly sliced
3 spring onions [scallions], trimmed and finely chopped
1 teaspoon dried dill

DRESSING

½ teaspoon prepared French mustard
6 tablespoons olive oil
2 tablespoons white wine vinegar
½ teaspoon paprika
½ teaspoon salt
¼ teaspoon black pepper

To prepare the dressing, in a small mixing bowl beat the mustard into the olive oil with a fork. Gradually beat in the vinegar and add the paprika, salt and pepper.

In a medium-sized serving bowl, combine the Danish blue and Cheddar cheeses, the red pepper, spring onions [scallions] and the dill.

Pour the dressing over the mixture and, using two large spoons, toss well to blend. Serve at once.

Egg and Spinach Salad

This fresh green salad makes an ideal light meal — and will taste even better if it is accompanied by thick slices of French bread and butter.

4 SERVINGS

¼ teaspoon black pepper
½ teaspoon salt
⅛ teaspoon cayenne pepper
1 teaspoon prepared mustard
5 hard-boiled eggs
1 large garlic clove, crushed
2 fl. oz. [¼ cup] tarragon vinegar
4 fl. oz. [½ cup] olive oil
1 tablespoon lemon juice
1 small lettuce, washed, trimmed and the leaves separated
12 oz. fresh leaf spinach, washed, trimmed and drained
8 large radishes, washed, trimmed and thinly sliced
1 tablespoon finely chopped fresh chives
1 small green pepper, white pith removed, seeded and very finely chopped

In a small bowl, combine the pepper, salt, cayenne and mustard. Slice the eggs in half and scoop out the yolks. Rub the yolks through a strainer into the mustard mixture and stir in the garlic. Chop the egg whites and set them aside.

In a small bowl, beat the vinegar, oil and lemon juice together. Gradually pour into the egg yolk mixture, stirring constantly until the dressing is blended.

Arrange the lettuce, spinach, radishes, chives, green pepper and egg whites in a large salad bowl. Pour the dressing on top and, using two large spoons, toss the salad thoroughly.

Chill the salad in the refrigerator for 30 minutes before serving.

Fagioli con Tonno
WHITE BEAN AND TUNA SALAD

An attractive Italian salad, Fagioli con Tonno may be served as a refreshing first course on its own, or as part of a colourful antipasto.

4 SERVINGS

1 lb. canned white haricot beans, drained
1 medium-sized onion, finely chopped
½ tablespoon white wine vinegar
2 tablespoons olive oil
1 teaspoon lemon juice
1 garlic clove, crushed
1 teaspoon salt
½ teaspoon black pepper
2 tablespoons chopped fresh basil or 1 tablespoon dried basil
7 oz. canned tuna fish, drained and coarsely flaked
6 black olives, stoned

Put the beans and onion in a medium-sized serving dish. In a small bowl, beat the vinegar, olive oil, lemon juice, garlic, salt, black pepper and basil together with a fork.

Pour the mixture over the beans and onion and toss well together.

Arrange the tuna fish and olives on top of the bean mixture and serve the salad at once.

Garlic Salad

An easy-to-make and strongly flavoured dish, Garlic Salad may be served as a first course or, accompanied by lots of bread and butter, for a light but satisfying summer lunch.

4 SERVINGS

6 large lettuce leaves, washed and shaken dry
8 medium-sized hard-boiled eggs, sliced
4 medium-sized tomatoes, washed and sliced
1 small green pepper, white pith removed, seeded and finely chopped
8 anchovy fillets

DRESSING

1 tablespoon finely chopped fresh parsley
¼ teaspoon dry mustard
¼ teaspoon salt

Garlic Salad is an enticing mixture of lettuce, eggs, tomatoes, green pepper and anchovies, covered with a strong garlic dressing. Serve with crusty bread for a special summer meal.

¼ teaspoon freshly ground black pepper
3 garlic cloves, crushed
4 tablespoons olive oil
1 tablespoon tarragon or red wine vinegar
1 tablespoon lemon juice

Arrange the lettuce leaves on a large serving plate.

Place the egg and tomato slices on the lettuce leaves, in alternating layers, beginning from the centre of the dish. Sprinkle on the chopped green pepper. Roll up the anchovy fillets and arrange them on the outer edge of the dish.

To make the dressing, in a medium-sized mixing bowl, combine the parsley, mustard, salt, black pepper and garlic cloves. Slowly beat in the olive oil, vinegar and lemon juice. Combine the mixture thoroughly and pour it carefully over the salad so that all the ingredients are thoroughly coated.

Place the salad in the refrigerator to chill for 15 minutes before serving.

Grapefruit and Avocado Salad

A delightfully fresh-tasting dish, Grapefruit and Avocado Salad may be served as an elegant and unusual first course to a summer dinner party, or as part of a summer buffet.

4 SERVINGS

2 large ripe avocados, halved and stoned
2 teaspoons lemon juice
1 large grapefruit, peeled, white pith removed and roughly chopped
1 head of chicory [French or Belgian endive], trimmed, washed and chopped
2 teaspoons sugar
3 tablespoons French dressing

Using a teaspoon, carefully scoop out the avocado flesh and place it in a medium-sized mixing bowl. Reserve the avocado shells.

Add 1 teaspoon of the lemon juice, the chopped grapefruit, chicory [French or Belgian endive] and sugar and, using a fork, mash the ingredients carefully together until they form a relatively smooth mixture.

Stir the dressing into the avocado mixture. Spoon the mixture into the avocado shells and sprinkle over the remaining lemon juice. Place the filled avocados in the refrigerator and chill them for 30 minutes.

Remove the filled avocado shells from the refrigerator and serve them immediately.

Jellied Veal

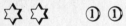

This dish should be prepared the day before it is to be served to allow the stock to set to a firm jelly which can be turned out easily.

6-8 SERVINGS

2 lb. lean leg of veal, boned
8 streaky bacon slices
1 small onion, thinly sliced
1 celery stalk, chopped
1 carrot, scraped and chopped
  bouquet garni, consisting of 4
  parsley sprigs, 1 thyme spray and
  1 bay leaf tied together
$\frac{1}{4}$ teaspoon salt
$\frac{1}{2}$ teaspoon black pepper
1 pint [2$\frac{1}{2}$ cups] water
5 fl. oz. [$\frac{5}{8}$ cup] white wine
$\frac{1}{2}$ oz. gelatine
6 artichoke hearts, cooked and
  thinly sliced
$\frac{1}{2}$ large cucumber, trimmed and cut
  into $\frac{1}{4}$-inch slices

Tie the veal into a neat shape, if necessary. Tie the bacon slices neatly around the meat. Place the veal, onion, celery, carrot, bouquet garni, salt and pepper in a large saucepan. Pour the water and wine into the pan and bring to the boil over high heat. Cover the pan, reduce the heat to low and simmer for 1$\frac{1}{4}$ hours, or until the veal is very tender.

Remove the pan from the heat and allow the veal to cool slightly in the cooking liquid. Remove the veal from the pan and set it aside on a board.

Strain the cooking liquid into a saucepan and bring it to the boil. Remove the pan from the heat and sprinkle the gelatine over the liquid, stirring until it has dissolved. Set aside to cool.

Rinse a 3-pint [1$\frac{1}{2}$-quart] soufflé dish with water. Set aside.

Cut the veal into 1-inch cubes and arrange one-quarter of them in the soufflé dish. Arrange a layer of one-third of the artichoke heart slices on top. Then place one-third of the cucumber slices over the artichokes. Repeat the layers until all the ingredients are used up, ending with a layer of veal.

Pour the cooled cooking liquid over the mixture and place the dish in the refrigerator. Chill for at least 4 hours, or until the jelly [gelatin] is very firmly set.

Remove the dish from the refrigerator. Dip the base quickly in hot water and place a serving dish, inverted, over the top. Reverse the two — the jellied veal should slide out easily. Serve cold.

Beautiful Jellied Veal makes the perfect centrepiece for that special summer buffet. Make it the day before for worry-free entertaining.

Kokonda

Kokonda is a spicy fish dish, ideal for a summer meal. Serve with a tossed green salad, and a well-chilled white wine.

6-8 SERVINGS

1$\frac{1}{2}$ lb. white fish fillets, cooked,
  skinned and roughly chopped
4 tablespoons lime juice
4 tablespoons fresh lemon juice
4 oz. fresh coconut, grated
1 red pepper, white pith removed,
  seeded and shredded
1 green pepper, white pith removed,
  seeded and shredded
2 bananas, thinly sliced
4 medium-sized tomatoes, chopped
1 cucumber, peeled and diced
4 oz. canned pineapple, drained and
  chopped
DRESSING
1 teaspoon salt
$\frac{1}{2}$ teaspoon black pepper
$\frac{1}{8}$ teaspoon ground cumin

1 green chilli, finely minced
1 garlic clove, crushed
5 fl. oz. [⅝ cup] sour cream
2 tablespoons single [light] cream

In a medium-sized dish, mix together the fish and lime and lemon juices. Set the mixture aside to marinate in a cool place for 1 hour, basting occasionally.

Drain the fish, reserving 1 tablespoon of the marinade. Place the fish in a serving bowl and add the remaining salad ingredients. Toss well and set aside.

To make the dressing, place the reserved marinade and the dressing ingredients in a small mixing bowl.

Blend the dressing thoroughly and pour it over the salad. Toss well and chill in the refrigerator for 1 hour.

Remove the salad from the refrigerator and toss well before serving.

Macaroni and Herring Salad

A deliciously different salad, Macaroni and Herring Salad makes a tasty meal served with crusty bread, or it may be served as part of a summer buffet.

4-6 SERVINGS

4 oz. cooked macaroni
2 celery stalks, chopped
2 oz. mushrooms, sliced
3 pickled herring fillets, drained and chopped

2 hard-boiled eggs, sliced
1 medium-sized potato, cooked and chopped
2 tablespoons olive oil
1 tablespoon red wine vinegar
1 teaspoon salt
½ teaspoon black pepper
½ teaspoon dried dill
¼ teaspoon cayenne pepper
¼ teaspoon turmeric
½ teaspoon ground cumin
1 teaspoon ground coriander
4 fl. oz. [½ cup] mayonnaise
5 fl. oz. [⅝ cup] sour cream

Arrange the macaroni, celery, mushrooms, herrings, eggs and potato in a large salad bowl and set aside. In a small bowl, combine the olive oil, vinegar, salt, pepper and dill, beating until they are well blended. Pour the dressing over the salad mixture, tossing with two large spoons until the mixture is coated. Place the bowl in the refrigerator to chill for 1 hour.

Just before serving, remove the salad from the refrigerator.

With a wire whisk, beat the cayenne, turmeric, cumin and coriander into the mayonnaise, whisking until the ingredients are well blended. Stir in the sour cream. Spoon the mayonnaise mixture over the salad ingredients and, using two large spoons, mix well until the salad mixture is thoroughly coated. Serve at once.

Mushroom and Asparagus Mayonnaise

Mushroom and Asparagus Mayonnaise makes an excellent accompaniment to cold roast meat.

4-6 SERVINGS

8 oz. button mushrooms, wiped clean and thinly sliced
1 lb. asparagus, cooked and sliced into 1-inch pieces
8 fl. oz. [1 cup] mayonnaise
1 tablespoon chopped fresh chives
2 hard-boiled eggs, thinly sliced

DRESSING

6 tablespoons olive oil
2 tablespoons white wine vinegar
¼ teaspoon salt
¼ teaspoon black pepper

First prepare the dressing. In a medium-sized mixing bowl, combine all the dressing ingredients, beating until they are blended. Add the mushrooms and set aside to marinate for 30 minutes.

Add the asparagus, mayonnaise and chives to the mixture and mix well, being careful not to mash the asparagus.

Transfer to a large serving dish. Garnish with the egg slices and serve.

Kokonda is a spicy fish salad from Africa. Serve with lots of bread and salad for a summer lunch.

Pork and Vegetable Salad

This fresh-tasting, colourful salad makes an ideal summer lunch, served with crusty rolls and butter. A lightly chilled rosé wine, such as Rosé d'Anjou, would be a good accompaniment.

4-6 SERVINGS

14 oz. green beans, cooked, drained and halved
4 medium-sized tomatoes, roughly chopped
2 medium-sized potatoes, cooked and chopped
1 large green pepper, white pith removed, seeded and thinly sliced
4 spring onions [scallions], trimmed and chopped
1 garlic clove, crushed
4 cooked beetroots [beets], sliced
6 black olives, halved and stoned
2 courgettes [zucchini], cooked and sliced
1 lb. lean cooked pork, cut into ½-inch cubes

DRESSING

5 fl. oz. [⅝ cup] sour cream
2 tablespoons lemon juice
4 tablespoons mayonnaise
1 teaspoon salt
1 teaspoon black pepper
2 teaspoons paprika
2 teaspoons prepared French mustard
2 tablespoons finely chopped fresh chives

Place all the salad ingredients in a large salad bowl and set aside.

In a small mixing bowl, beat all the dressing ingredients together with a wooden spoon until the mixture is smooth.

Pour the dressing over the salad and, using two large spoons, toss the salad until it is thoroughly combined. Chill the salad in the refrigerator for 1 hour before serving.

Potato, Egg and Anchovy Salad

This strongly flavoured salad may be served with cold roast poultry, such as chicken or turkey.

4 SERVINGS

1 lb. new potatoes, cooked, peeled and sliced
½ head of fennel, trimmed and thinly sliced
1 tablespoon finely chopped fresh chives

2 hard-boiled eggs, chopped
10 anchovy fillets, chopped
1 tablespoon red wine vinegar
2 tablespoons olive oil
½ teaspoon salt
½ teaspoon freshly ground black pepper
4 fl. oz. [½ cup] mayonnaise
1 tablespoon capers

In a medium-sized mixing bowl, combine the potatoes, fennel, chives, eggs and anchovies together.

In a small mixing bowl, beat the vinegar, oil, salt and pepper together with a kitchen fork. Stir the mayonnaise into the dressing. Pour the mayonnaise mixture over the potato mixture and toss well with two forks until the ingredients are well mixed. Transfer the salad to a glass salad bowl. Sprinkle the capers over the salad.

Serve immediately or chill the salad until it is required.

Radish, Celery and Cucumber Salad

This crispy, crunchy salad makes a palate-tingling hors d'oeuvre, which may precede almost any main course. Since the radishes are left whole, small ones would be best; if you have large ones, either cut them in half or quarter them.

3-4 SERVINGS

8 oz. radishes, trimmed
4 celery stalks, trimmed and cut into ¼-inch lengths
½ small cucumber, peeled and diced
3 oz. [½ cup] cashew nuts
½ teaspoon chopped fresh chervil or ¼ teaspoon dried chervil
½ teaspoon chopped fresh tarragon or ¼ teaspoon dried tarragon
¼ teaspoon salt
½ teaspoon black pepper
4 fl. oz. [½ cup] sour cream
1 tablespoon mayonnaise
1 tablespoon cider vinegar

In a medium-sized serving bowl, combine the radishes, celery, cucumber, cashew nuts, chervil and tarragon. Set the bowl aside.

In a small mixing bowl, combine the salt, pepper, sour cream, mayonnaise and vinegar, beating well with a fork until they are well blended. Pour the dressing over the vegetables and, using two large spoons, toss well until they are thoroughly coated.

Serve immediately or chill until it is required.

Rice Salad with Garlic Sausage

A tasty dish from southern France, this Rice Salad with Garlic Sausage makes a colourful addition to any table. Serve with crusty bread and chilled white Provençal wine.

4-6 SERVINGS

4 oz. [⅔ cup] long-grain rice, washed, soaked in cold water for 30 minutes and drained
1½ teaspoons salt
½ teaspoon black pepper
3 fl. oz. [⅜ cup] mayonnaise
2 teaspoons chopped fresh chervil or 1 teaspoon dried chervil
½ red pepper, white pith removed, seeded and chopped
2 hard-boiled eggs
1 small lettuce, outer leaves removed, washed, separated into leaves and shaken dry
1 x 8-inch garlic sausage, cut into ¼-inch slices

Put the rice in a saucepan. Pour over enough water to cover the rice and add 1 teaspoon of the salt. Bring the water to the boil over moderately high heat and cover the pan. Reduce the heat to very low and simmer for 15 to 20 minutes or until all the liquid has been absorbed and the rice is cooked and tender. Remove the pan from the heat. Transfer the rice to a large mixing bowl and set it aside to cool for 5 minutes.

Meanwhile, in a small mixing bowl, combine the remaining salt, the pepper, mayonnaise and chervil.

Pour half the mayonnaise mixture over the rice and add the red pepper. Using two large spoons, toss the rice mixture until it is well coated with the mayonnaise. Set the mixture aside to cool completely.

Meanwhile, cut the eggs in half, remove the yolks and add them to the remaining mayonnaise mixture. Mash the yolks into the mayonnaise mixture with a wooden spoon and beat well. Spoon the mayonnaise mixture into the cavities in the egg whites.

Arrange the lettuce leaves in a salad bowl. Pile the rice mixture on top of the leaves, then arrange the sausage slices and filled egg whites around the rice.

Serve immediately.

This sumptuous Rice Salad with Garlic Sausage makes an ideal centrepiece for informal summer entertaining.

4 tablespoons finely chopped fresh
  parsley
2 tablespoons finely chopped fresh
  mint
1 medium-sized onion, finely
  chopped
3 spring onions [scallions], trimmed
  and finely chopped
1 lb. tomatoes, coarsely chopped
1 teaspoon salt
2 teaspoons black pepper
2 fl. oz. [¼ cup] lemon juice
3 fl. oz. [⅜ cup] olive oil
10 lettuce leaves, washed and
   shaken dry
4 tomatoes, quartered

In a medium-sized mixing bowl, mix
together the wheat, 3 tablespoons of the
parsley, the mint, onion, spring onions
[scallions] and chopped tomatoes until
they are thoroughly combined. Set the
bowl aside.

In a small mixing bowl, combine the
salt, pepper, lemon juice and oil, beating
well with a kitchen fork. Pour the dressing
over the salad and toss well, using two
large spoons.

Line a medium-sized salad bowl with
the lettuce leaves and arrange the salad
in the middle. Garnish with the tomato
quarters and remaining parsley before
serving.

Turnip and Date Salad

*A really unusual combination of flavours,
Turnip and Date Salad is an ideal accompaniment to cold roast poultry, such as duck
or chicken.*

2 SERVINGS
2 tart eating apples, peeled, cored
  and diced
2 teaspoons lemon juice
1 medium-sized turnip, peeled and
  finely grated
14 fresh or dried dates, stoned and
   coarsely chopped
2 teaspoons sugar
2 fl. oz. single cream [¼ cup light
  cream]
1 small carrot, scraped and finely
  grated

Place the apples in a medium-sized salad
bowl and sprinkle over the lemon. Add
the grated turnip and the chopped dates
and sprinkle over 1½ teaspoons of the
sugar. Stir carefully with a wooden spoon
until the ingredients are thoroughly
combined.

Pour in the cream and, using two
large spoons, toss the salad until the
ingredients are thoroughly coated. Gar-

Sweetcorn Salad

*Piquant Sweetcorn Salad is an imaginative
yet easily made accompaniment to hamburgers or grilled [broiled] steaks.*

4 SERVINGS
1 lb. canned sweetcorn, drained
1 small green pepper, white pith
  removed, seeded and finely
  chopped
3 canned pimientos, drained and
  finely chopped
4 spring onions [scallions], trimmed
  and finely chopped
2 fl. oz. [¼ cup] olive oil
1 tablespoon white wine vinegar
1 bay leaf
2 teaspoons soft brown sugar
½ teaspoon salt
½ teaspoon black pepper
⅛ teaspoon Tabasco sauce
1 teaspoon dry mustard
1 garlic clove, crushed

Place the sweetcorn, green pepper,
pimientos and spring onions [scallions] in
a decorative salad bowl and toss well
with two forks until they are thoroughly
combined.

*Colourful Sweetcorn Salad makes a
delicious accompaniment to grilled
[broiled] hamburgers.*

In a small mixing bowl, mix together
the olive oil, wine vinegar, bay leaf,
sugar, salt, pepper, Tabasco sauce,
mustard and garlic until they are well
blended.

Pour the dressing over the sweetcorn
mixture and stir well to mix. Set aside at
room temperature for at least 2 hours.
Remove and discard the bay leaf before
serving.

Tomato and Wheat Salad

*This tasty tomato salad with wheat and
fresh mint is an adaptation of a traditional
Arab dish. It may be served as an hors
d'oeuvre or as an accompaniment to spiced
meat or chicken. Cracked wheat is available
from most health food stores.*

6 SERVINGS
8 oz. [1⅓ cups] cracked wheat,
  soaked in cold water for 20
  minutes and drained

nish the salad with the grated carrot and sprinkle over the remaining sugar.

Serve immediately.

Wurstsalat

GERMAN SAUSAGE SALAD

One of the classic German first courses, Wurstsalat may be made with any combination of cooked German sausages — we would suggest a combination of garlic sausage, salami, cooked frankfurters or bratwurst and ham sausage but it's up to you! Serve with a well-chilled white wine and rye or pumpernickel bread.

4-6 SERVINGS

1 lb. mixed cooked German wurst, sliced
1 medium-sized green pepper, white pith removed, seeded and sliced

The unusual combination of ingredients in Turnip and Date Salad makes a nutritious and tasty dish.

1 medium-sized red pepper, white pith removed, seeded and sliced
1 onion, thinly sliced and pushed out into rings
4 fl. oz. [½ cup] French dressing
2 small gherkins, halved

Arrange the wurst, green pepper and red pepper decoratively on a serving plate. Scatter over the onion rings. Pour over the French dressing and garnish with the gherkin halves.

Place the plate in the refrigerator to chill for 30 minutes before serving.

Cabbage and Sesame Seed Salad

A salad with an unusual flavour, Cabbage and Sesame Seed Salad is particularly good served as a side dish with cold beef or ham.

4 SERVINGS

12 oz. white cabbage, coarse outer leaves removed, cleaned and finely shredded
4 oz. bean sprouts, washed and drained
4 tomatoes, quartered
2 medium-sized carrots, scraped and finely grated
1 medium-sized avocado, peeled, stoned and chopped
1 tablespoon butter
2 tablespoons sesame seeds
6 fl. oz. [¾ cup] French dressing

Place the cabbage, bean sprouts, tomatoes, carrots and avocado in a medium-sized serving bowl and set aside.

In a small saucepan, melt the butter over moderate heat. When the foam subsides, add the sesame seeds and cook, stirring frequently with a wooden spoon, for 3 to 5 minutes or until the seeds are golden brown. Remove the pan from the heat and transfer the seeds and cooking juices to the salad.

Pour the French dressing over the salad and, using two large spoons, toss well. Serve immediately.

Mange-tout Salad

An adaptation of a Chinese recipe, crunchy Mange-tout Salad may be served as an accompaniment to cold meats, or as part of a Chinese meal.

4 SERVINGS

4 dried Chinese mushrooms, soaked for 30 minutes in cold water
1 tablespoon vegetable oil
6 oz. canned bamboo shoots, drained and thinly sliced
12 oz. mange-tout [snow peas], trimmed
1 celery stalk, trimmed and cut into 2-inch pieces
1 teaspoon salt
½ teaspoon sugar
1 teaspoon white wine vinegar

Drain the mushrooms. Strain the soaking liquid and reserve 1 tablespoonful. With a sharp knife, cut the mushrooms into thin slices.

In a large frying-pan heat the oil over moderately high heat. When the oil is hot, add the mushrooms and bamboo shoots and cook them, stirring constantly, for 2 minutes.

Add the mange-tout [snow peas] and celery to the pan and cook, still stirring, for 2 minutes. Sprinkle the salt, sugar, vinegar and reserved soaking liquid over the vegetables. Cook the mixture for a further 2 minutes or until the liquid has evaporated.

Remove the pan from the heat. Pour the vegetable mixture into a medium-sized serving dish and set aside to cool. Cover the dish with plastic wrap and place it in the refrigerator to chill for at least 1 hour before serving.

Picnic Salad

This fabulous salad makes a filling picnic meal served with either French bread or rolls and butter. Or serve it at home on its own as a first course to a main meal. To take the salad on your picnic, place it in a plastic bowl and cover with an airtight lid — it is preferable to chill the salad in the refrigerator for at least one hour before the journey.

6 SERVINGS

1 lb. lean cooked chicken meat, diced
6 oz. canned or frozen sweetcorn, drained or thawed
4 oz. small button mushrooms, wiped clean and thinly sliced
1 medium-sized avocado, peeled, stoned and coarsely chopped
2 medium-sized peaches, blanched, peeled, stoned and coarsely chopped
5 oz. [2 cups] cooked long-grain rice, or 6 oz. cooked diced potatoes, cold
2 shallots, finely chopped
2 tablespoons finely chopped fresh chives
1 tablespoon finely chopped fresh parsley

DRESSING

6 fl. oz. [¾ cup] mayonnaise
2 fl. oz. double cream [¼ cup heavy cream], whipped until thick but not stiff
1 tablespoon lemon juice
2 teaspoons curry powder
1 teaspoon salt
½ teaspoon freshly ground black pepper
⅛ teaspoon cayenne pepper

First make the dressing. In a large mixing bowl, beat the mayonnaise, cream and lemon juice together with a wooden spoon. Add the curry powder, salt, black pepper and cayenne pepper, and stir well to blend.

Add all of the salad ingredients and, using two large spoons, toss the salad thoroughly. Cover the bowl with aluminium foil and chill the salad in the refrigerator for at least 1 hour before serving, tossing it occasionally.

Salade Mimosa

LETTUCE HEART, CELERY AND WATERCRESS SALAD

An attractive French composite salad, Salade Mimosa makes a lovely hors d'oeuvre. It may also be served as an accompaniment to grilled [broiled] steaks or lamb chops.

4 SERVINGS

2 lettuce hearts, washed and shredded
½ bunch watercress, washed, shaken dry and roughly chopped
2 celery stalks, trimmed and chopped
3 fl. oz. [⅜ cup] French dressing
2 hard-boiled egg yolks, roughly chopped

GARNISH

2 oranges, peeled, white pith removed and segmented
2 teaspoons olive oil
1 teaspoon white wine vinegar
1 banana, peeled and thinly sliced
1 tablespoon lemon juice
10 green grapes, halved and seeded
1 tablespoon single [light] cream

In a medium-sized mixing bowl, combine the lettuce hearts, watercress, celery, French dressing and egg yolks. Using two large forks or spoons, toss the ingredients until they are well mixed. Transfer the lettuce mixture to a glass serving dish.

In a small mixing bowl, combine the orange segments, oil and vinegar. In another small mixing bowl, combine the banana and lemon juice and in a third small mixing bowl, combine the grape halves and cream.

Arrange the fruits and their dressings decoratively over the top of the lettuce mixture.

Serve immediately.

Cabbage and Sesame Seed Salad is a refreshing mixture of cabbage, bean sprouts, tomatoes, carrots, avocado and sesame seeds.

Sweet Pepper Salad may be served as an attractive hors d'oeuvre.

Sweet Pepper Salad

This Romanian salad can be served as an hors d'oeuvre, as a salad course or as an accompaniment to a meat dish.

4 SERVINGS

4 green peppers
4 red peppers
6 tablespoons white wine vinegar
2 tablespoons medium-dry sherry
1 tablespoon Worcestershire sauce
6 tablespoons olive oil
1 teaspoon salt
¼ teaspoon black pepper
2 teaspoons sugar
1 teaspoon paprika
12 stoned black olives
8 oz. cream cheese, cut into cubes

Wash and dry the peppers. Halve and remove the white pith and seeds. Cut the peppers into quarters. Half-fill a saucepan with water and bring to the boil. Add the peppers and blanch for 3 minutes. Drain and dry on kitchen paper towels. Cool.

In a large mixing bowl, combine the vinegar, sherry, Worcestershire sauce, oil, salt, pepper, sugar and paprika. Taste and add more seasoning if necessary.

Put the peppers into the marinade and turn and mix until they are coated with the dressing. Cover and marinate for 24 hours in the refrigerator.

To serve, place the peppers in a shallow bowl or dish. Spoon a little of the marinade over them. Place the olives and cheese over the top and serve.

Tomato and Fish Salad

This adaptation of a classic South American recipe makes an unusual and refreshing first course.

4-6 SERVINGS

2 lb. mackerel fillets, skinned, cooked and cut into 1-inch pieces
juice of 4 lemons
1 teaspoon salt
1 teaspoon black peppercorns, crushed
4 fl. oz. [½ cup] olive oil
6 tomatoes, blanched, peeled and chopped
2 large onions, thinly sliced and pushed out into rings
4 oz. [1⅓ cups] stoned green olives
½ teaspoon dried oregano
2 green chillis, finely chopped
6 fl. oz. [¾ cup] dry white wine
1 avocado, halved, stoned, peeled and thinly sliced

Place the mackerel in a shallow serving dish and pour over the lemon juice. Sprinkle over the salt and pepper and set aside for at least 4 hours.

In a medium-sized mixing bowl, combine the oil, tomatoes, onions, olives, oregano, chillis and wine and stir well.

Drain off and discard the lemon juice from the fish and pour over the oil and wine mixture. Chill the salad in the refrigerator for 30 minutes. Remove the dish from the refrigerator and garnish with the avocado slices. Serve at once.

Wilted Lettuce Salad

In this American salad, the crispness of the bacon contrasts well with the texture of the lettuce.

4 SERVINGS

1 round [Boston] lettuce, outer leaves removed, washed and shaken dry
6 streaky bacon slices, chopped
2 fl. oz. [¼ cup] white wine vinegar
1 teaspoon sugar
½ teaspoon black pepper
6 spring onions [scallions], trimmed and chopped

Tear the lettuce leaves into medium-sized pieces and place them in a large bowl.

In a frying-pan, fry the bacon over moderate heat for 6 to 8 minutes or until the bacon is crisp. Scrape the bottom of the pan frequently to prevent the bacon from sticking. Using a slotted spoon, remove the bacon from the pan and drain it on kitchen paper towels.

Stir the vinegar, sugar, pepper and spring onions [scallions] into the frying-pan. Bring the liquid to the boil. Remove the pan from the heat and pour the contents over the lettuce.

Toss the salad to coat it with the dressing. Sprinkle over the bacon and serve.

Yorkshire Ploughboy

This traditional English salad should be eaten as an accompaniment to cold meat.

4-6 SERVINGS

1 small red cabbage, coarse outer leaves removed, washed and very finely shredded
1 onion, thinly sliced
1 tablespoon dark treacle or molasses
2 tablespoons white wine vinegar
½ teaspoon prepared mustard
½ teaspoon salt
½ teaspoon black pepper

Place the cabbage and onion in a large serving dish.

Place the treacle or molasses, vinegar, mustard, salt and pepper in a small bowl and stir with a metal spoon until the ingredients are well blended. Pour the dressing over the cabbage mixture and, using two forks, toss the salad until it is thoroughly combined. Serve at once.